750

DATE DUE

OCT 1 8 '63	NOV 9 1983		
NOV 6 '63			
NOV 27 '63			
JAN 28 '64			
JAN 3 0 '64			
FEB 1 3 '64			
MAR 3 0 '64			
JAN 4 '65			
JAN 4 '65			
JAN 1 4 '65			
DEC 9 '66			
MAR 21 '66			
APR 1 8 '66			
APR 2 7 '66			
MAY 2 '66			
JAN 23 '67			
JAN 24 '67			
OCT 11 1979			

GAYLORD   PRINTED IN U.S.A.

WORLD OF COLOR

An Introduction to the Theory
and Use of Color in Art

by

Martin Koblo

Translated by Ian F. Finlay

McGraw-Hill Book Company · New York · Toronto · London

© 1963 Oscar Brandstetter Verlag KG
Library of Congress Catalog Card Number 62-17513
35265

Printed in West Germany

Foreword

Color occupies an important place in our lives. It is, in fact, impossible to imagine that we could do without it. Through their color content and their expression of color, objects live and become real.

Colors achieve their full effect only as a result of contrast. Red would not be conceivable without green; there would be no black without white. Color indicates what is bright and what is dark, it divides what is near from what is distant, and can equally well represent chaos or order.

Surrounded by the thousands of shades that nature showers upon us in rich profusion, the artist should become through his works the interpreter of a world – a world of color. For this, a knowledge of technical matters and of the most important principles in the realm of color is necessary. The selection of colors and binding media also requires a certain technical skill, which in turn depends on the purpose in hand.

We know that color is a child of light. Each impression the eye receives is determined by a difference in the wave length of light rays, causing us to perceive a corresponding color. This abstraction is accomplished by pigments which possess the physical property of absorbing light in such a way that they reflect back to us the colored rays that are proper to them, namely, blue, red, yellow, and so forth. The natural color of a body, its coloring matter, is formed in this way.

The practical application of these pigments to the various techniques used in painting will be explained in this book. The numerous black-and-white and color illustrations serve as guides and examples.

Apart from the theory of color, there are also instructions for combining colors (color harmonies). The possibilities for using color are considered again in the light of the various techniques.

Artistic and technical hints that have proved successful in practice may also be taken as a guide for creative work. This book is not, however, intended to help solve artistic problems; this lies outside its scope. Those who work with color should themselves choose and perfect the technique suitable to their nature, which is possible only through constant diligence and perserverance. This book has been written as a result of practical experience and is therefore intended to be a guide and adviser for solving practical problems. It is profusely illustrated with color plates and examples of a wide variety of techniques; and it is the author's hope that it may prove a valuable work of reference for the creative artist.

Martin Koblo

Contents

III. History

WORLD OF COLOR

Plate I

Vincent Van Gogh (1853–1890) ''Portrait of a Zouave'' Stedelijk Museum, Amsterdam
This Dutch-born master of the Postimpressionist period in France represents the more emotional
and intuitive side of that art. He was also much influenced by Japanese woodcuts and transferred
their purity of design and color into the technique of oil painting. (See also Plate II.)

Plate II

Vincent Van Gogh (1853–1890) "Landscape at Auvers"
Marshall Field Collection.

Plate III

Frans Hals (1581–1666) "La Bohémienne," Louvre Museum, Paris
Along with Rembrandt, Frans Hals holds a place of prime importance among Dutch painters of the
seventeenth century, and he is particularly noted for his lively figures and quick accurate brushwork.

Plate IV

Paula Modersohn-Becker (1876–1907) "Still Life with Pitcher and Bottle," Kunsthalle, Bremen.
Although this German painter came under the influence of Gauguin and Cézanne,
she developed her own individualistic style which combines great simplicity with expressive color
and texture, and was a forerunner of Expressionism. (See also Plate V.)

Plate V

Paula Modersohn-Becker (1876–1907) "Peasant Child," Kunsthalle, Bremen.

Plate VI

Johannes Vermeer (1632–1675) "The Girl," Mauritshuis, The Hague
Vermeer's style is marked by a pervading serenity and order. His extraordinary
skill in representing space and the technical perfection and luminous quality of his work,
make him one of the most important painters.

Plate VII

Henri Toulouse-Lautrec (1864–1901) "Dance Hall in Paris."
Colored lithograph. Toulouse-Lautrec was highly influenced by the style
of the Japanese colored woodcuts and produced masterpieces of colored lithography depicting
the theater and night life of the nineteenth century.

Plate VIII

Henri Toulouse-Lautrec (1864–1901)
Poster of the Singer and Dancer, Jane Avril.

Plate IX

Edouard Manet (1832–1883) Model for the "Bar at the Folies Bergères" Dijon Museum, France.
During the last years of his life, this master of French
impressionism very often turned to the pastel-crayon, and his portraits and flower pieces of that
period are among some of the most beautiful products of pastel painting.

Plate X

Kitagawa Utamaro (1753–1806) "Two Girls" Woodcut.
Utamaro belongs to that group of outstanding Japanese painters who specialized in the field of
delicate colored woodcuts, and is recognized as one of the great masters among the printmakers.

Plate XI

Tsunoda Kunisada (1786–1864) "Portrait of an Actor."
Colored woodcut. Even during his lifetime,
this Japanese painter belonged to the greats in the realm of art in his country. The contrast
of colors and the greatly simplified lines give his prints a poster-like touch.

Plate XII

Paul Cézanne (1839–1906) "Vase with Tulips." Art Institute of Chicago
Originally influenced by the impressionists, after 1885 Cézanne turned more and more away from this
kind of art, and is now often recognized as the progenitor of modern painting. (See also Plate XIII.)

Plate XIII

Paul Cézanne (1839–1906) "The Hut"
Kunstmuseum, Basel.

Plate XIV

Paul Gauguin (1848–1903) "Tahiti Women" Museum of Western Art, Moscow.
The work of this French Postimpressionist painter and graphic artist, along with that of Cézanne
and Van Gogh, has been of tremendous importance in the formulation of various twentieth century
schools. Gauguin is noted for his great feeling for the emotional and symbolic power of color.
(See also Plate XV.)

Plate XV

Paul Gauguin (1843–1903) "Landscape in Brittany."
Private Collection, Switzerland.

Plate XVI

J. M. W. Turner (1775–1851) "Rocky Bay with Figures."
This outstanding British landscapist had a great influence on his contemporaries and later on the
Impressionist painters of France. His sense of movement and atmosphere were of
great importance in the development of open-air painting.

What is Color?

Today virtually everyone knows that wave motions exist in the ether and that radio stations transmit extremely delicate electrical forces throughout the world. The expression "wave length" has in this way come to mean something to modern man. Sound is likewise a movement of the air, although its propagation is measured in very much smaller wave lengths. The same applies to light waves which are, however, measured only in millionth parts of a millimeter. Consequently, light is caused by vibrations of the ether, which in turn produce various sensations on our retina, depending on whether the number of vibrations is large or small. If we were to examine the colorless light of the sun or the light produced artificially by a lamp, we would find that this white light is by no means a homogeneous concept. It is, rather, a collection of various wave lengths. The human eye can perceive rays that range in length from about 400 to 700 millionths of a millimeter. Each millionth part of a millimeter means a difference in color, since each color in the spectrum is associated with a quite definite wave length.

If we wish to break down white sunlight into its individual constituents, we pass it through a narrow slot and a triangular piece of glass called a prism. The ray is refracted or bent in the prism and, in place of the narrow strip of light, a colored band of pure and full colors is formed; this is the so-called solar spectrum.

The seven colors of the rainbow, namely, RED · ORANGE · YELLOW · GREEN · BLUE · INDIGO · VIOLET, together with all their perceptible transitions, form the most important group of colors in the prism. The lowest number of vibrations of light causes us to perceive red, and the highest number of vibrations results in violet. Corresponding to their number of vibrations, the remaining colors lie between these two extremes. Purple, which intrinsically has all the properties of a color of the spectrum, cannot be seen in the spectrum. The combination of both ends of the spectrum, that is to say red and violet, results in purple.

The sum of all the colors of the spectrum, as also observed in the rainbow, results in white. Using a second prism, the spectrum can again be dissolved, and we obtain white light as before. A further aid is the color circle which, in

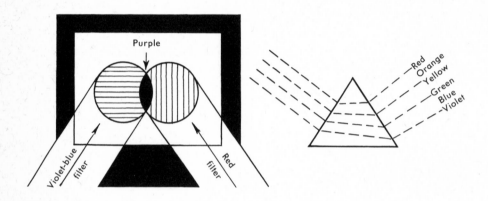

light-mixing experiments, confirms the theory that all colors when mixed together do, in fact, result in white. If the color circle is made to rotate rapidly, all details of the colors are obliterated, and we see merely a gray area. According to the laws of physics, white and gray = colorless. A gray strip, laid alternately on white and black grounds, now appears to us as gray and now as white. The strip will always be considered as "white" when it lies on a black ground, but as gray on a white ground. It is clear from this that our eye alone cannot in any way establish a given degree of brightness; rather, it can only determine the contrast to surrounding areas. An example of this occurs in the well-known painting "The Man in the Golden Helmet" by Rembrandt. The brightest light on the helmet, which sparkles like a gem, becomes a dull gray as soon as a pure white is placed directly beside the "painted light." These tests, at any rate, prove that the concepts "white" and "gray" merely express difference in the degree of brightness. They differ only in that a white body reflects light almost completely, while a gray body "swallows" the same fraction of each color of the spectrum. The more light a gray body destroys in this way, the darker is the gray we perceive, the final result being a black. It is, to be sure, impossible to find an absolute black among pigments, since even the deepest black velvet still reflects a fraction of light. In any case, the physicist looks upon white, gray, and black as being colorless.

What do we mean by the term "color"?

By means of a further test using the color circle, we come closer to answering this question from the physical point of view. We remove the orange field from the circle, covering it with a black surface. When this modified color circle is made to rotate rapidly, the individual fields of color are once again mixed. Now, however, we do not obtain a gray shade but a blue one. If the purple be removed in the same way, the result is the "mixture" green. If the blue-violet is missing from the circular scale, we obtain yellow; on the other hand, if the yellow is missing, we have blue-violet. Even with the complete absence of the color blue, the circle would allow us to perceive a blue shade, because the orange is suppressed. This is explained by the fact that the wave lengths for green and violet combine and produce a color chord which we call blue. The colors removed from the color circle in these tests are called complementary colors. They are: RED and GREEN, ORANGE and BLUE, YELLOW and VIOLET. There is, of course, a great number of intermediate shades between these large and most important groups of colors, with a relevant complementary color for every individual wave length in the spectrum. This is confirmed if we look for a certain time at yellow or red light. After closing our eyes, we see the corresponding complementary color. In the case of red light, we see a green spot and, in the case of yellow, a violet spot. The normal eye is accustomed to white light, which contains the color constituents red, blue, and yellow. It therefore always looks for the complementary color corresponding to the colored light.

A further experiment with a "color circle" consisting of only two complementary colors or with two projectors that, by means of suitable filters, radiate the colored light superimposed, again produces the result white-gray. This type of light blending is described as ADDITIVE, since in this case the luminous impressions are added. The retina can undertake color mixing with the same result, if the colors to be mixed are arranged in the form of a mosaic and the eye is no longer able to differentiate the finer details. In the case of the SUBTRACTIVE mixing of light, there is no pure optical blending of the colors. It is, in this case, rather a combination of coloring matters, i. e. of pigments, which has taken place on a base. It follows from this that such subtractive mixtures always tend towards a somewhat impure, blackish shade, in contrast to additive mixing in which the colors are always whiter in character than their constituents. A mixed color will appear all the more pure and intensive, the more the colors to be mixed are related to one another. The mixing of complementary colors according to the additive method always results in WHITE, while in the case of their substractive mixing the result is BLACK. Much more could be said about the colors of the spectrum and the possibilities of mixing them. Since, however, all paintings depend on the color pigment, the coloring substance, we will now consider the nature and use of these colors. The scale of the colors of the spectrum by no means exhausts the whole wealth of colors in nature. Colors such as pink, lilac, sky-blue, and the like are missing from it; these are formed if we mix white with the colors of the spectrum.

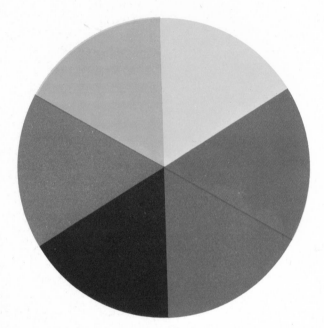

Color Circle

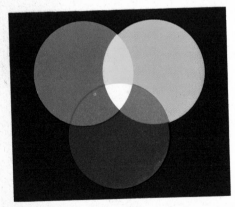

Additive Colors

Subtractive Colors

Ostwald and Goethe

Wilhelm Ostwald (1853–1932), the chemist and Nobel Prize winner for 1909, established the theory of color named after him. The aim to introduce his theory generally as a basis for teaching color was doomed to failure, since it is simply impossible to define color harmonies on a systematic basis. Anyone who is in direct contact with art as a creator or as a person with artistic sensitivity must realize from the start that such standardization cannot be possible. Research itself and the theory created by Ostwald with its necessary measurements doubtless form a worthy scientific achievement, but they cannot be used as a guide for artistic creation. Ostwald's theory has, of course, proved useful as an aid to industry in determining the value of a color. It remains restricted, however, to a region dissociated from creation.

To determine scientifically what colors can be considered as complementary and supplementing one another is possible only by using the pure colors of light obtained with the help of a prism. As soon as it is a question of using pigments, the results are contrary to the perceptions of practicing artists, even with the strictest application of method.

We know that the artist Paul Cézanne, who can with full justification be regarded as a magician with color, and whose artistic knowledge and sensitivity to color form an essential part of the painting of our time, preferred to leave white areas on his canvas, rather than fill them arbitrarily with color.

Personal sensitivity to color can be dispensed with when using the Ostwald color circle. We may compare such a desire to create a universally valid theory of harmony with the vain attempts to develop a perpetual motion machine. In any case the factor of independent force is lacking in an automatic theory of harmony that functions like the rise and fall of a thermometer, as is artistic feeling which cannot be built into any mechanism of whatever nature. It is an established fact that in all "non-harmonizing" colors the marked original contrasts can be cancelled by a uniform addition of black-white content. This is simply because the force or individual nature is removed from the color as a result of this addition. More tolerable total effects are created in this way, but only at the cost of a weakening of the color.

According to Ostwald, the hues are arranged in a group of twenty-four in the hue circle according to their similarity, with eight principal colors: yellow (1), orange (4), red (7), violet (10), (ultramarine) blue (13), ice blue (16), sea green (19), leaf green (22). The colors designated in this way correspond (apart from 10) to the colors of the solar spectrum with given wave lengths. The graduated white (w) and black (b) contents are designated by letters of the alphabet, which stand in the position of given hundredths. For example:

$$a = 89$$
$$c = 56$$
$$e = 36$$
$$g = 22$$
$$i = 14$$
$$l = 8.6$$
$$n = 5.6, \text{etc.}$$

The explanation of this theory lies in the following formulae:
The number indicates the color as such, the first letter the white content and the second letter the black content.

1 ie means a dull yellow
(1 = yellow, i = white content 14, e = black content 36)
13 ge means a medium blue
(13 = ultramarine blue, g = white content 22, e = black content 36)

It follows from this that the content of full color (f) is 50, in order to make the total 100.

$$f + w + b = 100$$

As already mentioned, the Ostwald theory can undoubtedly be used for **industrial standardizations,** and the names of the colors created by Ostwald are also reserved for this field. In art and aesthetics any overall and universally valid color harmony on a regulated basis has always foundered because of the multiplicity of color phenomena.

A generation before Ostwald, Goethe had studied color and its interpretation. With all the thoroughness of his search for new knowledge, it is understandable that the personality of the poet should have been directed more to the definition and interpretation of color as it appeals to the senses. Thus, for example, he wrote about the color yellow:

"Yellow possesses a joyful, cheerful, gently provoking property. This warming effect can be noted most vividly on viewing a landscape through a yellow glass, particularly on dull winter days. The eye is pleased, the heart expands, the mind is enlivened. A direct warmth appears to waft towards us. Yellow is the essence of magnificence and splendor."

These sentences by Goethe implicitly express a subjective poetic view, which nevertheless strikes at the heart of the matter. Concerning blue, the poet wrote as follows: "It always carries something of darkness with it, there is something contrary to charm and contentment in its aspect. Blue gives a feeling of coldness and reminds us of shadows. Blue glass shows objects in a melancholy light. Blue is the color of resignation, gentleness and lack of passion."

Goethe explained red in the following terms: "Red is the highest of all the phenomena of color. In the dark state this color appears serious and worthy, and in the bright state as charming and amiable. Viewed through red glass, the landscape appears sinister and frightening."

Concerning green, he wrote: "Calming, beneficial!"

In all such definitions and interpretations, it must not, however, be forgotten that the character of a color can change completely depending on its surroundings. A single color acquires its nature and value only through a second and additional color.

The Objective and Subjective Perception of Color

Hebbel once wrote in his diary: "We freeze if we see a white mass, we shiver before a white figure. Snow is white. We think of ghosts as being white, etc." These are concepts that form part of common human feeling. We speak of the discord and the harmony of colors. Aesthetes have created this idea, part of the general public has responded to it, so that to a certain extent it now follows a pattern. None of these aesthetic concepts can, however, be proved, and they remain relative. We must ask ourselves whether human perception is, after all, acute enough to understand and classify the multitudinous play of colors. We can, of course, measure color values, we can determine the effects of color, which in turn rest on bases of experience. We say that this or that combination of colors hurts us, that we feel an unpleasant sensation in our bodies on observing it.

15

The artist translates what he sees in nature and expresses it in his own way. To a certain extent he becomes the new creator of his own world, and in this way he forces the observer to see this newly created world with his own eyes. The untrained eye of the observer is thus transplanted into surroundings that may be foreign to it, offering new and unknown beauties. As a result of talent and constant training, the experienced eye of the artist recognizes color values and plays of color that remain hidden to the "layman." We speak of a reproduction of a subject as being "faithful to nature," the concept "faithful to nature" being on an absolutely relative plane. It may be that the majority of people agrees on the blue sky, green trees, and brown field, and also requires this formulation from the painter.

This formula may be true up to a certain point, so long as it stops at an elementary stage. When six or more painters conjure up the same subject on their canvas, there will be as many color interpretations as there are artists, providing the artists view the subject independently.

Denis Diderot (1713–1784), the French author and Encyclopedist, wrote in 1763: "There are natural relationships among colors, and these should not be neglected. The reflexes are a law of nature through which she seeks to restore the harmony of objects that has been shattered by contrast. If the colors of the rainbow are disarranged, the rainbow is no longer beautiful. Eliminate the blueness of the air which falls on the red of a beautiful face and spreads an imperceptibly gentle touch of violet on a few darker areas, and you will not be representing living flesh. If you have not noticed that when the extremities of a body are partly lying in shadow, the illuminated parts of the body appear to approach you, then you will never raise the contours of objects clearly from your canvas."

As long as it is a matter of a one-time color creation, as in "free painting", the expression of color is individual in nature, and expresses only an individual quality. The position becomes different as soon as color is to be used in a "reproductive" manner, be it in the form of fabrics, carpets, wallpapers, or in the design of decorative wall surfaces, or the like. Here, in the long run, only the color chord that is felt to be harmonious will prove successful, developed by the artist for reproduction after many tests and much practice.

It was said at the beginning of this chapter that the beauty of a color composition cannot be "proved", but the same or similiar experience by those who are particularly sensitive to color serves as a guide. It does, of course, seem difficult to define harmonious effects of color in the form of rules. If we speak of rules, we can certainly use basic conditions similiar to those for the creation of artistic form. Colors must therefore be brought into some relationship with one another, corresponding to the dynamic force inherent in each. The extent of the colored areas and the "force" of the individual colors require a proportional equilibrium. Among the multiplicity of variations, the following color harmonies may serve as a standard.

1. **The harmony of gray color**
   Use of gray shades with the same degree of variability;

2. **The harmony of equal shades or monochromes**
   Consists of the use of gradations of the same shade,
   for example, dark brown, medium brown, bright brown,
   dark blue, medium blue, bright blue;

3. **The harmony of different shades**
   Use of variegated colors having the same color values
   (with the same black and white content);

4. **The harmony of equal shades and different shades.**

The beauty or ugliness of a color is felt only through its surroundings. For this, the decisive factor is the area ratio between individual colors. Pure and intensive colors render harmony difficult, since each of them strives to be the determining force. Subdued or mixed colors are, on the other hand, easier to combine into a harmony since, as a result of mixing, a color relationship can be formed. A harmonious effect is always possible with related colors, in contrast to unrelated ones, that is those in a different key. These color chords, which we experience as beautiful, may be compared with beautiful chords in music. In painting we also speak of a "discord" of colors, or of a color dissonance.

4

Color as a Symbol

It is natural that legends and magic should have grown up around the mysterious world of color during the course of centuries. Color has played an important role, beginning in the kitchens of the alchemists in the earliest times
and extending down to the magical color of the postered walls of our day.
In the Middle Ages, for example, the use of pure and unbroken colors and that
of gold served not merely for painting and decorative purposes; colors had a
symbolic value as well. Objects and figures were intended to assume their
importance not only through their shapes, but also through their colors.
Thus we find a large measure of conformity in many medieval religious
paintings in their characterization of figures by the choice of color. The robe
of Judas the betrayer shows a preference for yellow, while that of the Virgin
Mary is painted in shining blue or green shades. An intensive red was very
often used for the cloak of the resurrected Christ; on the other hand, gray or
brown shades were in most cases chosen for the clothing of the male and female
servants and executioner's assistants.
We might have been inclined to interpret this uniformity of color as an emphasis on individual and particularly important persons, if the explanation
of the various colors in their symbolic importance had not been handed down
to us from the earliest times.
In this context we will quote a section from a letter by Van Gogh, in which he
gave an explanation of the paths he had taken. Color is particularly marked
as a symbol in Van Gogh's work, and this is confirmed by the following lines:
"Imagine I am painting an artist friend, an artist who dreams great dreams,
who works just as the nightingale sings, because this is his nature. This man
will be fair. I would like to paint into the picture all the love I feel for him. I
therefore first paint him as he is, as faithfully as possible, but that is only the
beginning. This does not mean that the painting is finished. I now begin to

color it arbitrarily. I exaggerate the fairness of the hair, I take orange, chrome, dull lemon-yellow. Behind his head, in place of the ordinary wall of the room, I paint infinity. I make a simple background of the richest blue, as strong as the palette can produce. In this way the illuminated fair head on the rich blue background gives the mysterious effect, through this simple combination, of a star in the dark ether." Apart from the artistic shaping and personal "handwriting" of the painter, color itself therefore becomes the interpreter of a work of art. It has, as Goethe described in his theory of color, the ability to affect the soul.

The symbolic interpretation given to colors varies according to the race and period of history. Nevertheless, we sometimes find many points of agreement in the symbolic interpretation of colors, irrespective of time and place.

White = innocence, purity, also coldness
Black = night, mourning, death, evil thoughts and deeds
Blue   = faithfulness, depth, chastity, woman
Green = hope, growth, also immaturity
Yellow = envy, hate, to the Romans the color of shame (sign of the plague)
Gold   = sun, riches, joy
Red   = blood, passion, man
Purple = ruler, majesty
Violet = mourning, resignation, dignity
Gray   = inferiority, age

In an old illuminated book dating from 1562 we find, among other things, the following characteristics, which are quoted in this context because of their originality:

Characters or secret signs, which are the characters or signs of the seven metals

These are the characters or signs that I have been able to find out. And I have had them printed here so that, if somebody comes across a book on black magic in which these signs occur, he will be able to understand it. They are quite common among those who do not like others to know about their art; they therefore designate the metals and substances by these signs, so that outsiders will not know them.

Sol. The sun signifies gold

Luna. The moon signifies silver

Venus. Signifies copper

Jupiter. Signifies tin

Saturnus. Signifies lead

Mercurius. Signifies quicksilver (mercury)

Mars. Signifies iron

Signifies steel.

There now follow other signs, which signify many types and colors of substances

☿ ♌.	Mercury	⚱ ⅄ ♁.		Antimony
♈.	Alum	☉.		This sign means Cinnabar
♊.	Verdigris	♏.		That is Stratum super Stratum
✢,	Vinegar	♃ℓ		This sign means Part
▽.	signifies Water	℥		as Recipe (that is, take)
△.	signifies Fire	♆.		This sign means Lapis Lazuli
♓.✳.☉.✳.⅄.∧.	Sal-ammoniac	♈.		Signifies Color of horses
♏Z.✛.✣	Common salt	♆✗		Signifies Violet-brown
♉.♆♉.♊.⬭.◠.	Sulfur	♃.		This sign means Bile pigment
☪.ᚠ.♇.	Salpeter	♃✗.		Signifies Aurum musicum
♄.♃.√.	Vitrol	$.		This sign means Saffron
☌.⬭.☐.⬭.♃.⅄.	Arsenic	♀.		This sign means Myrrhs tincture
		℞.		This sign means White lead
		∅.		Signifies ground Gold
		ℓ.		Signifies ground Silver
		♓.		Signifies Argentum musicum

Pigments

Painting by various techniques requires pigments which differ in their origin. Pigments are obtained mostly from chemical products that originate in part from the plant, mineral, and animal world.

Even if the technique of painting owes fascinatingly beautiful shades of color to advances in the chemical means of obtaining pigments, the brilliance of these pigments is often in contrast to their permanence. The unskilled use of many pigments can, in fact, result in a destructive effect because of chemical deterioration.

Centuries ago the painting of objects and rooms was an important activity. The fact that Egyptian paintings have in some cases been preserved very well down to the present day is due not only to the dryness of the climate or that they have been kept in sealed rooms, but much more to the knowledge of the painting materials that were used and which today still often serve as study material to those engaged in research on pigments.

The most beautiful paintings of the Egyptians, some still preserved in their original clarity, were carried out on walls that had a smooth coating of gypsum. The pigments used were mainly ocher (red and yellow), white (chalk, gypsum), black (soot), blue and green (copper), while the binding media consisted of animal glue, wax, and resin. This first ground for painting was further perfected in the painting of Egyptian portrait busts and of mummy cases. The wood to be painted on received a coating of chalk or gypsum onto which a further layer of animal glue was applied. The actual artist's colors were bound with honey, rubber, or egg. A coating of varnish, which was already known to the Egyptians, made the colors bright and vivid, so that even today many examples of this art are preserved in a state of undiminished freshness.

At that time no pigments were prepared in a finished state by factories. They had to be ground and provided with a binding medium by the painter himself. Renaissance painters used the same method for procuring their pigments as the ancient Egyptian artists had done many centuries before. They restricted themselves to a largish number of colored earthy minerals which were eminently suitable as painting materials and which have continued to be used up to the present (including Veronese earth and Sienna earth).

The individual preparation of pigments was a very laborious task. The minerals had to be pulverized and purified by repeated washing before the finished pigment could be obtained by mixing with the binding medium. The color grinder continued to be an important assistant in the larger studios right into the 19th century. The painter naturally learned all about the properties of his pigments by having to grind them himself.

Today with the help of microscopes and X-rays, we can investigate the layers of paint. Faulty chemical compounds can be discovered as exactly as the false use of varnishes, which can lead to the formation of cracks.

It would be presumptuous to underestimate the artistic merit of a perfect technique. Yet, unfortunately, a large number of masterpieces shows signs of decay that are not merely a result of time, but that often have been caused by lack of knowledge and skill in the choice of technical and chemical means, in other words by the incorrect composition of pigments.

22

Cremnitz White

This pigment has a high degree of covering power and takes only a short time to dry. Cremnitz white is the finest type of white lead. Since it has a tendency to turn yellow, it is preferably used for brightening yellow and red shades, in this way helping the "warm" colors to acquire great expressiveness. Cremnitz white, a poisonous lead oxide, is together with zinc white a very popular pigment.

Zinc White

This white pigment consists of pure zinc oxide, which is melted and then heated so strongly that it vaporizes. These vapors, brought into contact with the air, ignite and a pure white powder remains as the combustion residue. Zinc white has a lower covering power than Cremnitz white and also takes longer to dry, but the pigment can, as a result, be worked for a longer period by wet-in-wet technique. It is used for brightening green and blue shades and increases the expressiveness of these "cold" colors. Its glazing properties are greater than those of Cremnitz white, and it has a lesser tendency to turn yellow. When in the form of a powder, it always has to be kept well sealed, since it attracts moisture easily and becomes useless as a result.

Lithopone

Lithopone white has greater covering power than zinc white. In common with the latter, it is also suitable for artistic and commercial purposes. Lithopone is obtained from a mixture of zinc sulfide and permanent white. (The Barite form with a high covering power, insensitive to chemical influences, is seldom used as an oil pigment.) It can be mixed well with other pigments without danger of chemical decomposition.

Yellow pigments exist in fairly large number. They are mineral products or are produced chemically. The most common ocher shades come from yellow mineral pigments. They occur in nature from bright yellow to reddish-brown shades and are graded as desired by burning.

Ocher

These are pigments formed by the disintegration or weathering of rocks which contain a certain amount of iron oxide. Depending on the iron oxide content, the color range varies between bright yellow and brownish-red.

Ocher pigments, either burnt or not, may be used as required for artistic and commercial purposes. They are characterized by a high degree of resistance to light, can be mixed with any desired pigment, and are not subject to any chemical influences. These excellent properties caused them to be esteemed highly by the Old Masters. Even the extant cave paintings, dating from the Stone Age, as well as Egyptian paintings, show that these mineral pigments were used by those artists.

Apart from the pure natural product, it is also possible to obtain chemical products, that is oxide yellow pigments, which are equal to the mineral pigments in color intensity and fastness.

Depending on the raw material, the shades called **Caput Mortuum, Terra di Pozzuoli** and **English Red** are formed by burning. These are iron pigments whose residue, a beautiful red powder, depends on the degree of heating. (They are also prepared artificially.) These pigments, prepared from iron oxide alone, are among the most resistant and beautiful; they also include so-called **Indian Red.**

Vermilion is not light fast, dries slowly, but has good covering power.

It was often used, even in classical antiquity. It is a red pigment formed from a compound of mercury and sulfur (HgS).

Cinnabar (or vermilion pigment) occurs as a mineral in various parts of Europe, as well as in largish amounts in China and California. It is, however, no longer used as a mineral ore.

Most types of vermilion have a tendency to darken considerably with time. On old frescoes, which have been exposed to the light for long periods, a change to black has taken place. Many types of vermilion used as oil pigments also show a distinct blackening after long exposure to the light.

Chemical test: Pure vermilion evaporates upon heating, leaving no residue. Furthermore, it does not dissolve in water or alcohol. If a red solution is formed under these conditions, it indicates imitation vermilion.

Saturn Red is sensitive to hydrogen sulfide, but has good covering power. It is a fiery red oxide of lead (Pb_3O_4) which is changed into **Red Lead** (minium) on absorbing oxygen and being heated. It is used chiefly as a grounding oil pigment for anti-rust paints, since it is easy to spread and has a decidedly good covering power.

Saturn red is used in oil and watercolor painting, since the binding media increase its permanence. When exposed to the light as a dry powder, it turns black.

Carmine has a low resistance to light. It is a magnificent red pigment obtained directly from cochineal beetles (reared in Central America and Algiers).
It is also manufactured from coal-tar dyes (so-called adulterated carmine) and is then said to have a higher degree of light fastness than cochineal carmine.
Carmine is a favorite oil and watercolor pigment in spite of its poor resistance to light, since it is not exceeded by any other red lake in depth of color and brilliance.

Madder Lake

1. **Root madder lake** is fairly resistant to light, but does not cover. It is a dyestuff obtained from the dried root of the madder plant which has in recent times lost more and more of its importance for the manufacture of pigments. Today the pigment obtained from the madder root is generally used in a mixture with anthracene, a constituent of coal tar.

2. **Alizarin madder lake,** intensively bright, is manufactured solely from coal-tar dyes. It is, however, characterized by a higher degree of light fastness than the plant product, and has become indispensable as a glazing color.

3. **Rose madder lake** contains a high percentage of crimson, but fades after prolonged exposure to light.

In common with all lakes, the various types of madder lake are unsuitable for frescoes because of their poor resistance to light.
Numerous varieties of madder lake in a wide range of shades have appeared on the market. These lakes, for the most part, are not genuine alizarin products, but have been obtained from artificially produced dyestuffs similar to alizarin. Their degree of light fastness is slight. Pure madder lakes color neither water nor alcoholic solutions. If these liquids are colored, it is a sign of madder lakes that have been manufactured from coal-tar dyes.

Cobalt blue dries quickly, is resistant to light, and may be used in all painting techniques.

This color takes its name from its pigment, which is formed chiefly from cobalto-cobaltic oxide in combination with aluminium oxides. This compound, produced by burning a mixture of alumina with cobalt carbonates, is called by chemists cobalt aluminate. Cobalt blue is a thoroughly safe pigment.

Cerculean blue is resistant to light and may be used in all techniques. It has good covering power. It is a favorite greenish-blue pigment that consists chiefly of cobaltocobaltic oxide and is thus a compound of cobalt and tin.

Cobalt green or **zinc green** is reliable and is formed essentially by a combination of cobaltocobaltic oxide and zinc oxide. Although reliable, this color is not absolutely necessary on the palette, since similar shades can easily be obtained by mixing cobalt and brilliant chromium oxide green.

Ultramarine blue is reliable and has good covering power. As a natural mineral color the pigment is contained in lapis lazuli (Iran, China, Siberia). Up to the time of the manufacture of artificial ultramarine (in the first third of the nineteenth century), this color was obtained from the stone and was one of the most expensive pigments.
The ultramarine blue obtained artificially today, compared with the natural mineral pigment, has the same degree of reliability and is a very inexpensive color; it is also known as **permanent blue.**

Paris blue or **Prussian blue** has a particularly good coloring power, dries well, and is resistant to light.
It is obtained by combining iron with cyanogen (carbon and nitrogen). It is a decidedly transparent pigment, but is very sensitive to lime and cannot therefore be used in fresco and mineral painting. Its particularly good ability to mix should be emphasized.

Chromium Oxide Green

As the name implies, this is obtained from the oxide of the metal chromium, and is one of the most permanent pigments, having exceptionally good coloring properties.

Brilliant chromium oxide green is an especially beautiful fiery green pigment that owes its color to chromium, namely chromium hydroxide. Mixed with white, it is obtainable under the name **permanent green.**

Schweinfurt green is the name for a brightly shining green shade having good covering power. Obtained from a double compound of copper acetate and arsenate, this pigment is extremely poisonous. The brilliant pigment, although not very sensitive to light, is not compatible with sulfur pigments (cadmium yellow) and ultramarine. These mixtures blacken as a result of combining chemically. Pigments that have the same unstable properties and poisonous nature include **Emerald green, English green, Paris green,** or **Guignet's green.** Charming as their luminosity may be, these pigments should be used with great caution.

Indigo is used mainly as a watercolor pigment and is only moderately fast to light.
The indigo pigment is obtained from the sap of tropical plants. It has been used since earliest times, as a color in painting and for fabrics. Apart from the more customary blue indigo dyestuff, there are also red and brown indigo shades. Today indigo is also made chemically by synthesis from coal-tar products. In common with Paris blue, it is unsuitable for fresco and mineral painting.

Mineral blue (azurite) is obtained either by grinding azurite (a mineral) or artificially from a copper sulphate solution. It is a thoroughly unreliable pigment that discolors to a bright green when used as an oil color. It is, at most, used in certain places as a lime color for painting (Veronese green).

Green earth is obtained from products of decomposition and weathering of certain minerals (Lake Garda). It is olive-green and brownish-green in shade and can be used in all techniques. It dries relatively well, but has poor covering power.

Burnt green earth is obtained as an ocher-brown shade on burning green earth. It has lost much of its importance in contemporary painting.

Sepia is a pigment used most often in watercolor painting. It comes from the ink bag of the cuttlefish found in the seas around Europe, and is imported in various shades, mainly from Italy.

Asphaltum is a pigment from Syrian asphalt, which comes in hard glassy brown pieces from the Dead Sea. It is little used in oil painting, but has long been utilized in etching (as a ground) and in reproductive techniques.

As a painting color asphaltum has proved rather unsuccessful because of its poor drying properties. The surface dries relatively quickly, but the lower layers do not. Moreover, thickish layers of asphaltum have a marked tendency to form cracks, and so it is best used for glazing only.

Lampblack is a finely ground carbon (soot) that is obtained in the combustion of resins, oils, tar, and so forth (pine and lamp soot). Lampblack is processed primarily into **India ink.** The Chinese and Japanese have had a great deal of experience in the manufacture of India inks.

Bright cobalt violet is a magnificent pigment which, in addition to its high toxicity (arsenic), darkens with time.

Umber is a pigment obtained from ocher-brown earth. The intensive shade comes from the ferric hydroxide content. It owes its rapid drying ability to the presence of manganese. Umber tends to darken when used for oil painting.

Burnt umber with a deeper and warmer tone is a pigment that may be used in all techniques.

Cassel brown or **van Dyck brown** is one of the mineral colors and is, therefore, organic in nature (brown coal, containing iron oxide). Its coloring power fades after the intensive action of light, more quickly in watercolors than in oil painting. It has poor drying properties.

Bistre is a pigment used for watercolors. It is a very finely prepared lustrous form of soot having a dark brownish color. In light it changes basically to a weak gray shade.

In order to make India ink drawings "washfast", that is to say, insensitive to the influence of water, a two to three percent solution of potassium bichromate is added to the separately ground India ink. The drawing is then exposed to the light for a few hours. An addition of thirty percent formalin has the same effect, if an India ink that cannot be washed out is unavailable commercially.

Ivory black is the residue from the burning of waste ivory which contains sixty-six percent bone earth. Ivory black therefore consists of coal, which is organic in origin, together with ivory bone ash. The extremely fine size of the particles of coal gives an extremely deep black. Other types of bone (antlers) are often used instead of ivory for the manufacture of this pigment. In common with all black pigments, ivory black dries slowly.

So-called **Vine black** or **Frankfurt black** is obtained by carbonizing grape vines (dry distillation) as well as other non-resinous woods.

Graphite is used chiefly as a writing material in pencils. It is a mineral obtained in mines (Ceylon, Siberia, Urals). It is not generally used as a pigment in painting. A mixture of finely washed graphite with clay slip is used for the manufacture of pencils. The amount of clay added and the temperature used for calcining determine the degree of hardness.

Coal-tar Colors

A large number of artificial organic dyestuffs is made by chemical synthesis from substances obtained from coal tar. The dyestuffs obtained from tar are not very suitable for painting because of their low degree of light fastness. The artificial dyestuffs that are fastest to light include the anthracene dyes. Coal-tar products are best used for industrial purposes (dye factories and the like).

Aniline Dyes

This is a group of dyes which has as its basis aniline and materials other than constituents of tar. Although a series of aniline dyes has found its way onto the artist's palette, these dyes do not prove successful in the normal palette range, apart from their use for sketches in the applied arts and in a series of aniline watercolors for similar purposes.

Besides the customary names for pigments which have in the course of time become firm concepts, there is also a number of other names. These are either completely unimportant color variations or names of colors that have been derived from the place where the minerals or dyestuffs in question are obtained. Examples are Eosine red, Vienna red, Ceruleum, Berlin blue, mineral blue, Milori blue, mineral green, Venetian earth, and so forth.

Grounds for the Painting

We mean by this the nature of the surfaces which are covered or coated with pigment, that is to say, are painted on. Suitable for this purpose are wood, canvas, hard fiber sheets, plywood, cardboard, and paper. These materials have the property of absorbing liquid of any type. For this reason they have to be prepared previously as painting surfaces; the permanence of the painting depends on this, and — depending on the structure of the ground — the character of the painting. If we do not wish to use the types of canvas available on the market, which offer from coarse to very smooth surfaces, the materials mentioned can be treated suitably. This means that for physical reasons the wood, cardboard, or other pigment support is initially given a character in harmony with the natural expansibility of the pigments. Oil colors, after they are dried, have the property of expanding when heated, as does any other body, and of contracting when they cool. Such constant change can be undergone without a damaging effect on the painting (formation of cracks, and so forth) only if the ground likewise carries out these same movements which depend on temperature.

Convenient as it may be to work on industrially prepared canvas or pasteboard, a useful and intimate contact with the material will be developed by individual preparation of the ground. The advanced student will, moreover, be able to discover very quickly what ground suits his particular intentions and will prepare during the preliminary grounding work for the desired effect of his painting.

In the fourteenth and fifteenth centuries, massive wooden panels were often used as grounds; these were largely replaced by fabric during the ensuing centuries. Buckling of the wooden panels occurred to a marked extent, particularly in larger sizes. Today massive wooden panels made of poplar, linden, or willow have been replaced by sheets of plywood which are, however, to be recommended only for sizes up to about one meter. Wood fiber panels have proved more satisfactory in practice; both the rough and the smooth sides can be used as a ground for painting. For sizes up to half a meter, cardboard is also suitable, but only pasteboard should be used for this purpose, as the bright board made from wood pulp has too little stability. In order to prevent the board warping, it must be sized on both sides before applying the grounding mass. Strong drawing paper may also be used for sketches in oils. In this case, a coating with a thin solution of size suffices.

Colored grounds for painting were often used by the Old Masters. This was purely a question of individual preference. Leonardo da Vinci (1452–1519) wrote: "For the colors to which you wish to give beauty, you will always prepare an extremely bright undercoat or ground. This applies to translucent colors, for those which are not such are in no way helped by a bright ground." In the works of Paolo Veronese (1528–1588), a silver-gray ground was used. Raphael (1483–1520) no longer painted his large oils on white grounds, but on a medium shade. Both white and colored grounds are frequently found on one surface, large parts of the painting done on a dark surface and deliberately accented, brightly colored sections placed on a white ground. The transparent and shiningly colored Flemish paintings of the fifteenth century were carried out in small sizes on a white reflecting base. Rubens (1577–1640) later often used darkly shaded grounds, particularly for larger works, while his pupil, van Dyck (1599–1641) used these grounds almost exclusively.
In Tintoretto (1518–1594) and Correggio (1494–1534) we find red grounds that were later used almost without exception by numerous Italian painters of the sixteenth, seventeenth, and eighteenth centuries.
It follows from what has been said that up to now the color of the ground has been a personal matter. The more or less well preserved luminosity of colors on a white or colored ground is not much influenced by a bright or dark shade of the undercoat. The reasons for it must rather be sought in the nature of the oils and the oil content of the pigments.
Apart from wood, metal – that is, copper plates – was sometimes also used as a ground for paintings in the fourteenth and fifteenth centuries.
Basically all fabrics to be prepared must be stretched on wedged frames. Only in this way is it possible to smooth them out by subsequent stretching. Care should be taken that the wedged frame is not too narrow. The primed and dry canvas harbors considerable force and is quite capable of completely distorting a wedged frame that is too weak and even the frame of the picture itself. For this reason, in sizes larger than one meter, a reinforcing cross-brace is necessary. Suitable as fabrics are all closely woven types of material, such as sailcloth or

bleached linen; good unbleached cotton cloths may also be used for smaller sizes. Depending on the nature of the work and the sizes, a suitable choice of ground and fineness of surface will be made. The following main types of grounds come under consideration for painting:

Chalk ground
Half-oil ground or Half-chalk ground
Oil ground

Chalk ground

There should be used for this, if possible, a finely pulverized chalk (Champagne chalk), mixed in equal parts with dry zinc white powder. The mass is stirred with the continual addition of moderately warm size until the solution is free of lumps and can be painted on. This solution should be applied in three thin coats. An hour and a half should suffice for drying each coat. If the priming mass becomes too thick, it should be heated in a tub, possibly with the addition of some water.

Painting grounds prepared from chalk and zinc white powder are characterized by their permanence (no yellowing) and they preserve the luminosity of the pigment.

Gypsum ground

A type that occurs less often today involves the use of gypsum or marble dust as substances for a white ground. These materials guarantee a spotless ground because of their covering power. If a chalk size ground is about half a millimeter thick on a wooden panel, then islandlike spots are sometimes visible on it. These spots appear to be areas on the wooden panel which shine through the binding medium of the chalk ground, the size, and the uneven distribution of the chalk on the ground. In the case of thicker chalk grounds, about one and a half millimeters thick, this translucency disappears completely and a snow-white ground results, such as the Old Masters liked to use.

Half-oil ground or half-chalk ground

This type of ground likewise requires a preliminary sizing. Linseed oil varnish is added gradually in small amounts to the chalk ground paste as described above with its constituents: chalk, zinc white powder, and alum water. The mass, which becomes firm and tough, is then diluted with heated glue water so that it can be brushed on. The addition of linseed oil varnish results in a lesser absorptive capacity of the ground than with pure chalk. The nature of this pigment support also allows a more fluid manner of painting, but the drying time of the pigments is longer than with a chalk ground.

It is possible today to purchase factory-prepared emulsions.

To obtain the oil ground, which is also available ready-made in the trade, white lead is used. The fatter, or less absorptive, the oil ground is to be, the less the amount of chalk. Grinding is done with linseed oil varnish, and the ground is applied in several layers on the previously sized surface. Of course each coat must first be absolutely dry before a further thin layer is applied, the number of individual coats determining the degree of absorption of the pigment. Before painting is begun, the ground must be absolutely dry; this ensures brisk, smooth working. A longer drying time of the pigments must be expected, however, because of the non- or only slightly absorptive ground.

For the preliminary sizing of the ground, glue from leather waste has always proved successful, and is available from the trade in the form of beads. Before use, this size is allowed to swell in cold water for about six to eight hours. About three quarters of a liter of water is used for fifty grams of size. Once the size has swollen properly, it is heated while constantly stirring (preferably in a tub) until it has completely melted. One-tenth alum, or five grams (technically pure), dissolved in one-quarter liter of warm water, is added to the finished size. This alum solution makes the sizing more resistant. The luke warm size is applied with a broad flat brush. A canvas primed in this way must not be dried in the sun or by artificial heating. It is recommended that all wood and cardboard grounds be treated on both sides, so that a distortion of the sheets is avoided. In any case, care should be taken that the size is absolutely dry before the further priming layers are applied.

Smoothing the ground for painting

Ueven spots in the ground cannot always be avoided completely. They should nevertheless be removed by careful treatment with sandpaper. This is done by laying a piece of glass or sandpaper wrapped around a smooth box, and gradually smoothing the uneven spots by circular movements. This smoothing should, at any rate, be carried out prior to the final priming coat.

Binding Media for Oil Painting

The powdered pigments require a binding medium that mixes the small particles together, resulting in a mass which can be applied. The binding medium must, therefore, be able to change after a certain period into a solid body that encloses the particles of pigment and holds them fast. All pigments ground with rubber solutions or with glue water achieve solidity after the complete evaporation of water.

Pigments that have been ground with oil solidify through the drying of the fatty plant oils. As a result of this, the pigments are retained on the ground.

Investigations have shown that pigments ground **solely** with drying oil (siccative) have the maximum possible permanence. This type of painting does, of course, require a correspondingly long drying time, but there is less danger of cracking.

Practical conditions nevertheless require shortening of natural drying times, so that a further liquid is added to the pigments as a drying agent, apart from the oil as a binding medium.

The most important binding media used in the various types of painting are:

Linseed oil (unbleached)
Of all the drying oils, the most important in oil painting is linseed oil, obtained from the seeds of the flax plant. It has a bright golden yellow color. Colorless or bleached linseed oil gives the pigment a transient purer, more luminous appearance, but later tends to render the pigments yellow to a greater extent than the pure unbleached linseed oil.

Linseed oil varnish may be used as a priming agent and is formed by boiling together linseed oil and drying agents at temperatures up to two hundred fifty degrees centigrade. The linseed oil boiled in this way has a darker color than oil that has not been boiled. On the other hand, it has the property of drying much more quickly. (It can be used for all commercial paintings).

Nut oil

This is obtained from the kernels of walnuts and, as a fatty oil, has a similar composition and drying properties to linseed oil, but it becomes rancid more easily in air than linseed oil. Nut oil is very suitable, because of its bright color, for preparing artist's colors as well as for commercial use, although it is too expensive for this latter purpose.

Poppy oil

This oil is prepared from the seeds of the poppy plant. In common with nut oil, it becomes rancid more quickly than linseed oil and also dries very much more slowly. Poppy oil is also used with binding media for varnishing. This accelerates the drying process, and the pigment acquires a tough insensitive quality.

Hemp oil

This is pressed from the seeds of the hemp plant and has a bright yellow color when fresh. Its color soon changes, however, and it acquires a brownish shade. Hemp oil is remarkably liquid, but because of its dark color is suitable only for less sensitive pigments and for commercial painting.

Balsams

These always consist of a solution of certain fractions of resin in essential oil. They are, in most cases, viscous masses that are sometimes used in painting as an addition to the pigment, in order to give an increased degree of flexibility. As long as the essential oil contained in the pigment mass has not become separated by evaporation, the pigment will retain its flexibility. If it has evaporated, however, or become resinous in the course of time, cracks in the painting can no longer be avoided. The same is also true of **Copaiva balsam** which has, as a painting agent, a pleasant aromatic odor, although its tendency to dry as stone, coupled with the formation of cracks, renders it unsuitable.

Turpentines

Turpentine is obtained from various species of plants. Various types are available on the market, including German turpentine, manufactured from

36

local spruces, French turpentine, a product of the beach pine, Venice turpentine, obtained from the larch and others. The latter two have proved useful as diluents, half French and half Venice turpentine being mixed in a tub.

Resins

Resinous substances come from the plant kingdom. They are bright yellow to brownish-yellow in shade and can be dissolved in oil of turpentine. Since all resins lose their necessary elasticity after evaporation of the essential oil contained in them, only a brittle mass remains. The formation of cracks in the pigment is, therefore, a logical result.

Dammar resin

This resin comes from Southern Asia. It is obtainable on the market in the form of transparently yellowish and drop-shaped pieces. Its tendency to turn yellow is slight. Dammar resin is used both for the manufacture of oil colors and as a constituent of rapidly drying painting media. Solutions of dammar resin (dammar varnishes and dammar lacquers) give a firm, glass like, and colorless coating upon drying.

Mastic

The use of this resin of yellow color is restricted to retouching. It is also quite suitable as a final varnish.

Solvents

Pigments ground with oil can be diluted with the liquid **oil of turpentine,** which has no influence on the coloring material as such and evaporates after a short time. It is obtained from the crude resin of conifers and should, if its quality is correct, be a colorless to yellowish liquid. It should, if possible, be kept in a well sealed bottle made of dark glass (brown glass is the best). Pure turpentine is very sensitive to light and air. If a little be exposed to the light in a white glass bottle, it will be seen after a few weeks that the originally colorless liquid has taken on a yellowish shade, though the bottle has been well sealed. In the course of time this darkening gives turpentine a color resembling dark amber, and the liquid becomes increasingly viscous. If air is admitted, oil of turpentine changes into a thick lacquerlike substance that finally becomes resinous. Supplies of turpentine intended as solvents in painting should, therefore, not be stored for long periods. Once the liquid has become resinous, the sticky condition is transferred to the painting, and this state lasts unpleasantly long.

Genuine French turpentine, obtained from the balsam of the beach pine, has proved best for sound artistic work.

Many artists use **lavender oil** as a solvent when painting in oils. It is even more sensitive to oxygen of the air than oil of turpentine and, like **oil of spike** or **oil of spike lavender,** it is not to be recommended. While fresh lavender oil, so-called genuine lavender oil (obtained from the plant Lavandula vera), is almost completely colorless, a fairly intensive yellowish color soon develops in oil of spike through the action of ozone. The use of **oil of cloves** can be just as bad, particularly if a slow drying effect is desired in the interest of a wet-in-wet painting. Subsequent darkening of the pigments is likely, and the painting sometimes also remains in a sticky state for a long period. **Petroleum** is likewise not to be recommended as a solvent. The hardening of the pigment is in this case only partial, and this process can moreover take a very long time. Depending on the nature of the ground, it can also happen that the painting does not dry at all. A petroleum distillate, **turpentine substitute** (purified) can, however, be used as a solvent for paintings in which the drying process is to be prolonged. So-called **mineral spirits** can also be used safely as a solvent for dammar.

Painting Media and Siccatives

Oil colors, supplied to us in handy tubes by the dyestuffs industry, are usually of a thoroughly good quality, thanks to intensive chemical research and long years of an exhange of information between artists and manufacturers. The various colors meet such requirements as extremely fine grinding of the pigments and correct percentage additions of binding media and siccatives. The painter may, therefore, begin work without any addition of painting media, if the pigment completely satisfies his requirements as to flexibility and the ground chosen. Unfortunately, the age of such a tube of pigment often causes difficulties in this respect, so that it is not possible to use the pigment without a painting medium. A very good medium consists of a mixture of one-third French turpentine, one-third dammar, and one-third linseed oil. The use of oil of turpentine alone can result in poor stability of the pigments, if the contents of the tube do not contain sufficient binding medium.

By siccatives we mean drying agents that are intended to bring about particularly rapid solidification of the pigment. Since, however, every change in temperature causes a movement in the pigment surface, a strong tension will occur in the layer of pigment during a rapid artificial drying process, and in the course of time this will lead to the formation of cracks. We must therefore advise against the use of such siccatives for artistic work.

Mixing Colors

Any color can be altered by the addition of another color. The more white we mix with a color, the brighter will be its effect. As a result, the color also loses strength. If we mix black with a color, it too loses in luminosity, depending on the amount of black. The pure addition of white results in colors that come under the heading of "pastel shades", while the admixture of black gives the real value of the color a gloomy appearance. In musical terms, the minor keys can be mixed by a suitable addition of black. In the language of painting these processes are known as the "blending of colors." In the case of yellow and orange, a small addition of black suffices to give these colors a greenish appearance, while red is gradually transformed into brown by mixing with black. The three primary colors yellow, red, and blue are indivisible, that is, unmixed colors. Further colors may, however, be mixed from them, as can be seen from the color plate on page 41.

The artist distinguishes between warm and cold colors. By warm colors we mean all red and yellow shades, including the mixed color brown. Cold colors are blue and green.

By mixing in a further color, this warm or cold sensation can again be modified suitably, so that we speak of a warm or cold blue or green, and of a cold or warm red, yellow, or grey.

The characteristic effect and with it the color value of a pigment is determined by the proximity of other colors. If we do not wish to lose this characteristic effect, a limitation of the color by neutral outlines (black or white) is needed. For all those who do not yet have much practice in the mixing of colors, only a wide series of tests can lead to comprehensive knowledge in this field. It is

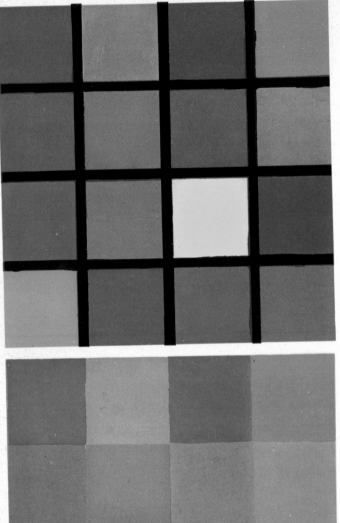

A color maintains its independence if it is separated from another color by an outline.

By mixing with white, the original force of a color is reduced. This color plate shows pastel shades formed by the addition of white.

The three Primary Colors
Indivisible, unmixed colors

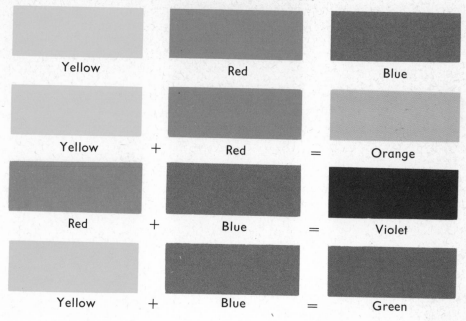

Yellow	Red	Blue
Yellow	+ Red	= Orange
Red	+ Blue	= Violet
Yellow	+ Blue	= Green

Two primary colors when mixed give a complementary color

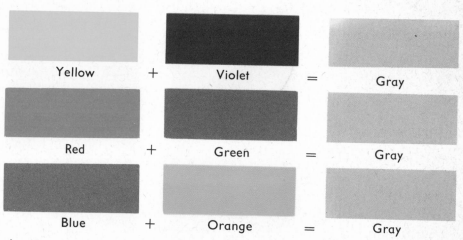

Yellow	+ Violet	= Gray
Red	+ Green	= Gray
Blue	+ Orange	= Gray

A primary color mixed with a complementary color gives a corresponding
gray shade

quite impossible to explain the multiplicity of gradations of color even approximately in words or pictures. The following list may serve as a guide. It will, however, vary as much as the percentage of one color which we mix with another.

Yellow and red	— ORANGE
Yellow and blue	— GREEN
Yellow and brown	— OCHER
Yellow and white	— BRIGHT YELLOW
Yellow and black	— OLIVE GREEN
Red and yellow	— ORANGE
Red and blue	— VIOLET
Red and brown	— RED-BROWN
Red and white	— PINK
Red and black	— BROWN
Blue and yellow	— GREEN
Blue and red	— VIOLET
Blue and brown	— DARK BROWN
Blue and white	— BRIGHT BLUE
Blue and black	— BLUE-BLACK

The resultant mixed shade will be as different as the individual colors in the tendency to be cold or warm.

The more a common degree of darkness or brightness is present in a color chord, the more the colors will blend. As colors are mixed to make them paler or darker, they lose in strength and become weaker. In this state of weakness the individual colors combine more easily than if they are strong and pure. The play of colors accordingly becomes monotonous, for the bright-dark effect, which we strive for in all color creations, is thereby destroyed.

When mixing colors, we must realize that the ground on which a color is to stand plays a decisive part in its effect. A bright intensive red, for example, will on a black ground display all its luminosity, while the same red on a white ground will manifest chiefly its degree of darkness.

42

Equipment
used in Painting

The success of an artistic work is not absolutely dependent on certain equipment. Let us not forget that all equipment we use in painting is nothing but an aid. This means that expensive and good painting equipment is all very well, but the success of a work is not absolutely dependent on it. There are many examples where artistically great work has been carried out with extremely modest equipment; on the other hand, a multiplicity of materials may have produced very poor results.

The painter Max Liebermann was once asked by a layman whether he did his quick drawings with a hard or a soft pencil. His answer was: "With talent!"

The brush

For watercolors a round marten-hair brush should, if possible, be chosen. These are more expensive than so-called "fish-hair brushes," but are, on the other hand, more permanent and more flexible. The term "fish-hair" is very curious, for brushes sold under this name are made from polecat or bear hair. The size of the watercolor and the method of working decide in each case the size of the brush. Numbers 1–3 are used mainly for fine commercial work. All watercolor work, including both graphic treatment and surface design, can be carried out with Numbers 4–10. Long-haired flat brushes can also be used for large watercolors. A round hair brush should have a fine point when wet. As soon as individual hairs become prominent or spread, difficulties and dirty work result.

The various types of brushes are not confined to one technique alone. Their use can, therefore, overlap. It is, for example, quite feasible that the finest oil

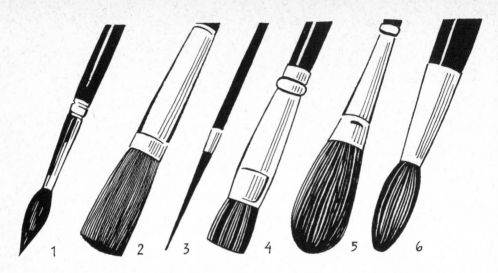

1 Marten-hair brush.   2 Marten-hair flat brush.   3 Stroke-brush.   4 Goat's hair brush.
5 Preliminary washing brush.   6 Goat's hair brush, round.

HAIR BRUSHES FOR WATERCOLOR PAINTING

and tempera painting can be done with a marten-hair brush which is normally intended for watercolors, or that, on the other hand, in special cases a bristle brush will be used in watercolor technique.

Brushes must always be cleaned properly after use. In the case of oil painting, this is done with lukewarm water and soap, while in watercolor techniques water alone suffices. After cleaning, the brushes should be dried with a sponge

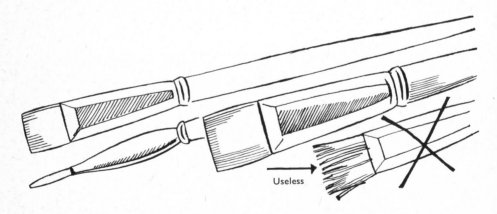

Useless

BRISTLE BRUSHES FOR OIL AND TEMPERA

and blotting paper, and only then placed in their containers. Under no condition should brushes be allowed to stand in water for a long period, since not only does this cause deformation of the brush hairs, but the glue may also dissolve and the handles swell.

The Palette

For watercolor painting the grinding surfaces (depressions) contained in each box of watercolors normally suffice. For smaller tempera works (sketches and commercial work) there are porcelain palettes of various sizes, while for mural painting a metal palette is preferred. For oil painting a light wooden palette, corresponding to the method and size of the painting, may be chosen; these are available in a wide variety of sizes. The palette is best cleaned immediately after use. When painting with oils, rags and spirits of turpentine are used, and the wooden palette cleaned in this way is rubbed with a few drops of painting medium. This restores the original gloss to the palette.

The Easel

For larger studio work a portable easel will be essential, on which a vertical adjustment of the ground for painting is possible. Working in the open air is not feasible without a good, preferably folding field easel. In a strongish wind the easel should be secured by placing sand, stones, etc. around the base of the legs.
Painting with watercolors does not require an easel. A firm base suffices, so that the work can be surveyed conveniently.

1 Palette cup or 'sticker'
2 Spatula for painting
3 Palette knife

The Painting of the old Masters

When we search far back into the past for old paintings that are well preserved, we meet with the works of the Egyptians, which tell us about the artistic skill and practices of this race. These paintings, after four thousand years, still appear in their full freshness. The colors owe their permanence not only to the effect of favorable climatic conditions or the darkness of the rooms in which they were housed, but also and mainly to the pigments used.

Today science has an undisputed share in investigating the painting techniques of the Old Masters. The microscope and X-rays show up the material of the former times with more clarity. This material can now be examined more accurately from a chemical point of view. We may observe the changes that chemical reactions bring about on the individual layers of a painting and even on parts of these layers. We thus discover what material is attacked or altered by the addition of certain substances.

In spite of these aids, we are lacking knowledge of a number of pigments used by the Old Masters. They also used a better varnish that protected their paintings more effectively against external influences. One reason for this may have been the many years of experience acquired by the master of an old painting school in the individual preparation of his colors. Despite all chemical progress and the reliability of certain manufactured colors, there are still many products on the market during the use of which the artist will encounter surprises. The methods of painting used by older painters and their artistic workshops are, in fact, characterized not only by composition and brushstroke, but to a large extent also by the pigments employed. The nature of the application of pigment in the lowermost layers of the painting shows us an amazing degree of technical skill, and the choice of superimposed colors implies a conscientious workmanlike practice. In many cases the Old Masters preferred a colored ground

Albrecht Dürer, Portrait of Elisabeth Tucher (1499)

instead of the otherwise customary white ground, the former corresponding best to the tone of the highest lights.

The first masters of oil painting considered that a white ground sustained beautiful and pure colors and accentuated their brilliance. Particularly deep shadings were thereby renounced. So far as the color force was concerned, these masters depended on balanced color values such as were offered by tempera, which had been used almost exclusively up to that time. It was gradually recognized, however, that oil color could enrich the color harmonies with more serious chords, and that the whole color range could now be extended by many shades. Leonardo da Vinci said more than once that one cannot paint real shadows and that it was therefore better to stick to the local colors. Leonardo was not alone in taking this view. His many practical tests, for the most part described in numerous diaries, give us today a fairly accurate picture of the nature of his creative process. Numerous anatomical studies and measurements, his laws concerning the use of atmospheric perspectives, in addition to his theory of light and shade, explain his works abundantly. He did research on which colors chiefly lose under the influence of atmospheric perspectives, and observed that the small lights and shadows dissolve and form a medium shade. Of interest, too, are his statements about the plastic effect of figures. It is stated with rare thoroughness that neither the full light side nor the full shadow side shows a body at its best in the roundness of its form. The plastic nature of a figure is most completely perceived if the eye is directed between light and shadow.

The more moderate and diffuse the illumination, the more beautifully do the shaded-off tones blend. Experienced in this way, Leonardo sought for an extended modeling scale. He shows the purest white only in the representation of the gloss, while he paints the shadow with light-absorbing glaze on a weak-colored ground. For his "under-modeling" he chose a neutral-colored gray on a brown ground. He also always stressed shape. The darkest shadows occur where the figures are closest together. "But color," he said, "should be everywhere. Only the complete lack of light, the darkness of night, is black." From these views of Leonardo da Vinci and from thorough investigations, there follow these technical hints regarding the painting technique of this Renaissance master:

o Predominantly white, yet always bright ground for painting

o Careful transparent brown underpaintings, with particular stressing of shapes

o Opaque further modeling

Later glazes.

48

Titian, Portrait of a Lady

6

49

The views of the Old Masters concerning the use of colors often reflected the teachings of their painting schools. It can be said that here it was a matter of pure recipe painting. The correctness of these recipes was believed in, and they were defended against others that were different. Titian (1477–1576) once said: "The colors have to be dirty!" In this view he was in opposition to colorism, namely the use of pure colors such as used, for example, by Albrecht Dürer (1471–1523) in his paintings. Titian's statement means an acknowledgment of tonal painting in which one total shade in the picture predominates, into which the colored accents fit harmoniously. This view of painting was later represented by Rembrandt (1606–1669), whose color scale was fairly narrow in range but who, nevertheless, conjured up with it the whole conceivable richness of light and color.

Right into the 16th century the original color in its various modifications was used for all plastic emphasis. A red, for example, plastically shaped, retains red as the basic color from the light right into the deepest shadow sections. The same applies to the modification of blue or green. The addition of dark color, here too, is chosen in such a way that the original color remains visible in the depth. A fullness of color is thus achieved, this being a particular characteristic of paintings of the Renaissance period.

The work of Peter Rubens (1577–1640), head of the Flemish school of painters, forms a climax in Baroque painting. The following method played a decisive part in the construction of his paintings:

o Ground in a yellowish-grey medium shade

o Outline of the figures and underpainting of the shadow sections in dark brown

o Semi-opaque further modeling of shapes in grey-brown

o Insertion of the bright local colors

o Glazes.

Among the host of masters of that period, we should like to single out Velásquez (1599–1660). He was one of those who occasionally ignored the traditional painting recipes, and laid the greatest stress on the development of a painting by the freest and most personal treatment of color and by an unheard-of breadth of execution. His influence on European painting extended into the 19th century. He preferred to choose a fiery red ground, as a result of which his paintings took on a pleasant warm tone from the start. Velásquez sometimes glazed with surprising boldness in opaque colors or placed opaque colors in glazed parts, using a rapid brushstroke.

Velásquez, Portrait of a Child

During the lives of the masters their manner of painting naturally changed in various ways as a result of successive developments or under the influence of contemporaries. Here it is less a question of change in views concerning the technical construction of their works, than of a development of character and growth of personality. For the expression of the personal element and for the struggle which this personality maintains with itself and the surrounding world, there are striking evidences from the beginning of all art up to the present day these evidences being the pictures themselves. We need only refer in this respect to the dynamic brushstroke of the aging Rembrandt or to the paintings of Van Gogh (1853–1890), which in their simplified view of shapes and original brushstroke are a complete declaration of war on convention. (See also supplement plates I and II)

Apart from this personal expression in the structure of the brushwork or of the personal handwriting, whole tone predominated in painting up to the beginning of the 19th century. From that time on, there took place a continual change which accentuated more and more the color and material nature of objects.

52

Color and Design

With increasing certainty in design perception and with the perfection of drawing, the first step towards modeling in color has been taken. Nevertheless, each person who penetrates the mysterious world of color for the first time enters a new country. We know from numerous observations that a child views color completely differently from an adult. The simplicity with which a child masters its surroundings graphically sometimes astounds us. With the same simplicity, unburdened by any concept of tradition, a child plays with brush and paint and creates its own world of color. The reasons for this may lie in the fact that the child lacks the conscious spiritual and artistic feeling for the creative process. Color is to it a toy, and yet the variety of colors certainly releases certain feelings in the child. With passing years, this simplicity is, in most cases, lost. People begin to see "correctly," want to draw and paint "correctly," and with this the small artistic creation ceases to be a symbol. It suddenly wants to be an image or likeness, to compete with what exists, and ambition arises, relegating the original feeling to the background. This is the point that distinguishes natural talent from training.

With this short introduction I should like to say that the adult himself, on the basis of his maturity and his extended power of judgment, has naturally set up a separating wall that is clearly characterized by the words prejudice and anxiety. Here too, of course, the exceptions prove the rule, but it is a firm fact that the first conscious meeting with color can, at least initially, remove the last vestiges of simplicity. This is simply because concepts have penetrated into our consciousness that are so firmly entrenched and are opposed to our desires. They all begin with the word "too." Too glaring, too bright, too dark, too poisonous, too dull, too powerful, and so forth. It is exactly the same with knowledge about objects, as preconceived and apparently irrefutable opinions, that can render working with brush and color difficult. An approved remedy against all influences of this type is the constant observation of nature. We know, of course, that a group of trees has millions of leaves; the human eye nevertheless sees only a section of this detail. At a certain distance, the perception of details is lost completely. There remains only the general shape. In this case the compactness of the group of trees can be perceived as a dynamic force. Simply and uncomplicatedly as the element from nature is represented, it nevertheless bears the stamp of something organic. A very similar position applies with the human figure. Here too, the uniformity of the view stresses the strength of expression. As an example of how the importance of compact form was emphasized in ancient Greece, there is a legend about a Greek sculptor who used to let his sculptures roll down a mountain to test them for vital function. The projecting parts of the body of the figures were liable to break and had therefore been created inorganically.

In the creation of color it is likewise a matter of simplification and compactness of the shapes.

Experts have coined the term "translate" for this. This transformation of what has been seen does not first take place at the moment of painting, but is an essential part of the whole creative process.

At the beginning of each creation in color stands man, who can to a certain extent be educated to a color culture through numerous examples of pictures by approved masters. This man has, however, acquired just as much influence on color sensitivity through his own innate properties, or vice versa; in other words, these properties influence his color sensitivity, and this explains the preference for quite definite colors. Apart from his delivery and brushstroke, a painter can also be recognized from the tone of his color, which is repeated in his creations.

The same applies to color as was said about the compactness of form. Nature, with its richness of color, forces itself on the painter in thousands of nuances. It is up to him to create order here, if his canvas is to document a new and original small world.

The two- and three-part color chord

In every pictorial creation it is necessary to strive for simplification of the form and the tonal values, and the same applies to the choice of colors. A composition is not improved as a result of a multiplicity of colors. A picture can become more harmonious and, at the same time, more expressive by using only two or three colors. Such a composition must, however, consist of colors that produce a harmonious effect. It may be entirely a question of complementary colors.

54

Martin Koblo, Color Composition

Examples of this are frequently found among the masterpieces of ancient and modern painting. Just think of the economical choice of colors in the unrivaled paintings of Rembrandt, of the mysterious chiaroscuro that can dispense with all brilliant colors. Also consider Vermeer's modest blue-yellow palette or, in the painting of our own time, the expressive works of Carl Hofer that were created with two or three colors. Apart from the simplification of shape, it is precisely these two shades, mixed with much gray and accented by the third, pure color, which form an absolute harmony.

Black and white

These two opposites always combine to form a harmonious chord. The gray resulting from them always fits in happily as a mean between bright and dark. Although the physicist considers neither black, white, nor gray, which comes between them, as a color, painting as a whole cannot be imagined without them. All colors, moreover, fit harmoniously into the black-white scale.

Plastic designing

Light, half-tone, and full-tone create the simulated third dimension. In order to give a body plastic form, we must start from a simple chiaroscuro effect. Light stands against shadow, and no claim is made at first on the gradations of the intermediate tones. These marked contrasts determine, even in the outline, the final pictorial statement, while the finer gradations of tone then lead to the necessary unity of the pictorial effect. The painter will, therefore, have to be clear first about the contrast effect, the chiaroscuro content of his chosen subject, for the correct contrast of color values determines the success of the work. Since, of course, light can penetrate into all corners of a space drawing without there necessarily being more than one source of light, the subject has to be broken down into its most essential contrasts. Light, through which our eye perceives the world of objects, is radiated by stronger or weaker sources. It meets dark bodies either as direct light or indirectly as reflected light. These bodies also appear brighter or darker depending on whether they are nearer to or farther from the source of illumination. These objects which allow the ray of light to pass very largely through their mass are transparent. They appear dark in external light and bright in light that passes through them. On the other hand, we find that nontransparent bodies are bright to external light, and dark (or shutting off light) if they stand between us and the light.

The simple chiaroscuro effect serves as the first step toward constructing a picture plastically

Light   Half-shadow   Full shadow   Cast shadow

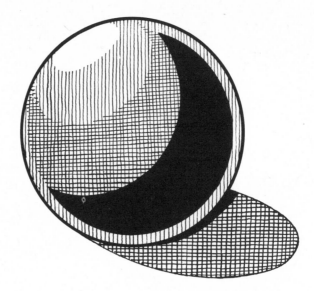

Introduction to composition

Composition means "putting together." In painting this means the arrangement of details according to formal conditions, symmetry or rhythm, light and shade, and colors. We must, therefore, place objects so that the picture acquires a unified construction. By picture, we mean here any work that requires artistic activity, beginning with the simplest drawing and passing via sketches in the applied arts up to the substantial pictorial work. The composition of a picture begins with the size which is chosen for it, since this is the basic requirement for its construction.

The sections of a picture should not merely stand side by side, since we wish to create a third dimension, namely that of depth, from the two-dimensional area. Care should always be taken with overlapping so that no shapes appear unbelievable because of others. Enough of a figure must therefore be present for the total form to be recognizable. It is better to separate similar basic forms from one another, since otherwise the picture loses in clarity. Too equal a

Objects placed next to one another do not form a composition.
For this, we must create depth, the third dimension

Lines running into one another do not make for clarity.
We therefore always seek to separate objects from one another by overlappings

In a still life it is preferable to show a view from above.
This creates plastic and convincing spatial design

59

treatment of tonal values in various parts of the picture cannot convey any idea of depth. For this reason, the objects in each composition must be set apart by suitable differences in tonal value and color.

If the vertical elements in a picture are to be stressed particularly, the hint or indication of a horizontal line can strengthen this intention, as can a diagonal

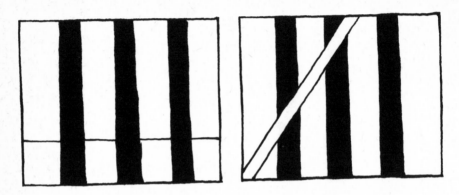

If we wish to stress the vertical elements in particular,
a horizontal or diagonal line will emphasize this intention

line. Conversely, the horizontal elements are accentuated by reference to the vertical elements. It does not matter whether it is a group of objects, a portrait, or part of a landscape. The laws of composition embrace all things.

If we study the composition of pictures by recognized artists, we can easily get the impression that all their paintings have been constructed according to purely geometrical preliminary sketches. It is rather that the construction of a picture is normally based completely on feeling. The fact that the observer subsequently finds certain geometrical intentions in a work does not alter the matter at all, or very little. Artistic perception is responsible for precisely this well-balanced construction of a picture and the fact that the forms and colors of individual portions are correctly arranged with regard to plane and color relationships. We must, of course, be clear about any picture's construction

Andrea Mantegna, Composition which is constructed from the oval and circle, and which shows a confluence of the main outlines

before beginning to paint. So-called composition sketches help to solve the problem of construction. These are cross-hatched or given bold contours, areas are planned, and attention is paid to vertical or horizontal stress. The composition sketch is, therefore, a plan according to which execution must be adjusted if pictures are to be created from inner conceptions. The pure view of nature which a painter wants to conjure up on his canvas must also be laid down before he begins work, in such a way that here too we can speak of a composition. Even before the first brushstroke has been made, the painter thinks out the whole construction. The finished picture appears before his mind's eye, with its limitations, center of gravity, and force of color. This creative process, which provides the concept for execution, differs from artist to artist, depending on the power of imagination. This preparatory work may be called a "translation of nature into patches of color."

Paul Cézanne, Composition for a picture in which the construction is determined by horizontal and vertical lines.

Pablo Picasso,
Composition in which the bright and dark values have been distributed with static accuracy

In the work of composition explained here, a concrete, that is, representational, method of interpretation is employed, for an abstract design can be based completely on a previously determined geometrical or mathematical construction.

Local Colors

By local colors we mean the actual color of an object, which can, of course, be altered completely by reflections and effects of illumination. If in painting we use local colors exclusively, then the color-modifying influence of light does not appear. The effect of objects is two-dimensional and expressionless. It is, to a certain extent, a question of painting or coloring in the shapes.

The extent of change in color produced by the action of light depends on the material of an object. Metal and glass, for example, are subject to a greater change than any dull-colored objects. This change may be so marked under strong light that only contrasts appear rather than local colors. Not only can a local color be worked up plastically and vividly by using darker and brighter shades of the same basic hue, but also in artistic design unrelated colors may be added. Similarly, in the shadow sections completely different colors can enliven the local color of an object. Impressionism contributed convincingly to this discovery. There are works in this style of painting which scarcely allow the material aspect of an object, and with it the local color, to express itself. The colored areas are dissolved, without destroying the unity of the picture. Neo-Impressionism goes even a step farther, in that all areas are completely dissolved and only the juxtaposition of small spots or points of color (pointillism) allows a picture to be formed on the canvas. The human eye supplements what is missing, so that, at a suitable distance from the picture, the shapes are again clearly recognizable.

Local color also changes according to the distance that separates the eye from the object. This is understandable because the intervention of layers of air can bring about this transformation in color values.

The color in the picture

It is important to know that the color prepared on the palette and applied to the painting surface does not correspond absolutely to the painter's idea. This is explained by the presence of other colors which also exert an influence. The very first brushstroke made on the canvas or paper will be decisive for all further tonal values.

Kandinsky, A composition stressing the filling of an area, rather than unity of the forms

The beginner can likewise be disappointed if he undertakes the experiment of converting a preliminary study in watercolors to the tempera or oil technique. The pigments of these techniques appear quite different, which causes this disparity. There is no other course than to translate the subject into the other technique. The fluid watercolor contrasts with the heavy and full shades of oil painting, apart from the usual thick application of color in the latter. Another error of the beginner lies in wanting to give a picture several accents. These accents not only cancel each other out, they also introduce a note of discord into the work. The same effect occurs if a color accent in the painting takes up too much space; in this way it becomes a stressed colored area that can unbalance the picture as a whole. We should not forget that an accent in painting is in the final analysis nothing but a colored stress, that is to say, it cannot appear again in the rest of the picture in this intensity. When, in an exceptional case, two color accents appear necessary, they must lie in direct proximity to one another, if the harmony of the picture is not to suffer as a result. A picture — and in this we include all techniques of painting — should always show a decided quality of color; it should not, however, under any circumstances have a gaudy or motley effect.

The Subject

What subject or motif is chosen is of no importance for a painting. Nevertheless, certain preferences for specific subjects cannot be denied throughout the centuries. The history of art shows us these preferences in changing succession. From painting that was concerned solely with religious subjects, a profane art developed only gradually, and it was a long time before pure landscape became the main subject of painting. Alongside this, there developed as special fields portrait art and still life. Today even the most unattractive or insignificant object can become the subject for a painting. It seems that such an object may be considered worthy of attention or even beautiful through the ability of the painter. One will naturally begin with simpler objects. After all, the hand and eye must be trained, and before a certain sureness in execution has been achieved by repeated practice and diligent study of color harmonies, we must limit the choice of subject to relatively simple arrangements or not too difficult landscapes. Portrait painting, and figure painting as a whole, should be reserved for later and more mature ability.

Color Table

This color table can serve only as a basis for combining colors. It is based on what has proved successful in practice. The twenty-two colors listed here can, of course, be supplemented by a further number of intermediate shades, the ratings given in this table possibly being liable to slight variations depending on subjective sensitivity to colors. This can be explained by the fact that even a slight addition of white or black to a color can change the degree of harmony. The color rating (1—4) is to be read off from the square which lies at the intersection of the colors in question, which are numbered 1 to 22 (both vertically and horizontally).

1 = very good color harmony
2 = good color harmony
3 = poor color combination
4 = very poor color combination

Since the table shows only the values when two colors are used, the addition of a third color will cause a corresponding change in the harmony ratings.

Example: bright blue + blue-green = rating 4, will give, in combination with black or dark brown as the third color, a good and harmonious color combination.

	White	Grey	Black	Violet	Wine-red	Carmine	Vermilion	Orange	Pink	Dark brown	Rust-brown	Ocher	Golden-yellow	Bright yellow	Bright green	Olive green	Dark green	Blue-green	Ultramarine	Cobalt blue	Grey-blue	Bright blue
Bright blue	1	1	2	2	2	2	3	3	3	1	2	1	2	4	4	2	2	1	1	2	4	■
Grey-blue	1	1	3	1	1	1	1	2	3	2	2	1	1	2	4	3	3	4	2	2	■	
Cobalt blue	2	1	2	2	2	3	2	2	3	3	2	1	1	1	3	4	4	4	3	■		
Ultramarine	1	1	3	4	4	4	3	1	2	3	1	1	1	2	3	4	4	3	■			
Blue-green	1	1	3	4	4	4	3	2	1	3	3	1	2	3	4	4	4	■				
Dark green	1	1	4	4	4	4	3	2	1	3	3	1	2	4	4	3	■					
Olive green	1	1	3	4	4	4	4	2	1	2	3	2	3	3	3	■						
Bright green	1	1	4	4	4	4	3	2	3	4	4	3	3	3	■							
Bright yellow	1	2	3	3	4	4	3	3	3	3	2	2	3	■								
Golden-yellow	1	2	3	3	3	3	3	3	3	2	3	3	■									
Ocher	1	1	1	2	3	1	1	1	1	1	1	■										
Rust-brown	1	1	1	4	3	2	2	2	1	1	■											
Dark brown	1	2	1	4	4	3	1	1	1	■												
Pink	1	2	3	4	4	2	1	1	■													
Orange	1	3	4	4	2	1	1	■														
Vermilion	1	2	4	2	1	1	■															
Carmine	1	2	3	1	1	■																
Wine-red	1	3	4	1	■																	
Violet	1	1	2	■																		
Black	1	1	■																			
Grey	1	■																				
White	■																					

Application of Color and Methods of Painting

Application of color

If we look back in time, into the workshops of the Old Masters with their systems of guilds, we observe that a work done for the church or a particular ruler was executed as a communal undertaking, just as was any commission to another guild. The master prepared the plans, the work bore his spirit, and yet the execution was a matter for many hands working with the master. In the painting of later periods, the artist alone creates a work within the four walls of his studio to testify to his talent and individual character in the galleries and exhibition rooms, and only then can it bring him judgment, appreciation, and commissions. This means that, in contrast to the old school of painting, the individual can now give more direct expression to his work and "handwriting."

Let us first turn to **painting in layers,** which was practiced almost without exception in the workshops of the Old Masters. Such works took a longer time to execute, since each individual layer of color had to be thoroughly dried before a new overpainting. Often more than ten overpaintings were necessary before the final and satisfactory solution was found. Apart from the construction of the picture and the special choice of colors, painting in layers does not show any special features in the handling of the brush. It can express a preference for specific color compositions, just as it also reveals technical refinements or inadequacies in mechanical execution. This includes the underpainting of figures or landscapes. In a well-considered construction the colors are applied thinly and smoothly, one upon the other, until the painting shows the intended effect. The details in the painting are delayed until the uppermost and final layers. Although painting in layers continued up to recent times, it has largely made way for **alla prima** painting. This is a technique that had already been used in the sixteenth century. This is confirmed by numerous well-preserved paintings dating from that time. In the seventeenth century, it was, among others, the lively paintings of Frans Hals (1581–1666) which made use of this technique. (See also supplement plate III)

By **alla prima painting,** we mean a method that provides for the application of color without underpainting the ground, in such a way that this application corresponds to the final effect of the picture. It does not matter whether part of the picture is first completed, or whether the whole subject is undertaken at once, from which the picture develops in wet-in-wet painting. Later corrections are quite possible, but for this the pigment must be properly dried. It is dangerous to paint over half-dried pigments, since when the pictures dries completely (often only after a longish period), chinks or cracks can appear on the surface. The works of the Impressionists would, for example, have been quite impossible without alla prima painting, as would all works that are finished in one operation. The subject is not important here. While painting in layers requires a thoughtful method of working, considering the relatively long drying time of the individual layers, alla prima painting requires a sure handling of the brush. Timidity cannot lead the beginner to his objective here, nor can excessive elan in execution that does not keep pace with ability.

Painting with glazes is a type of painting in layers that is likewise built up on an underpainting. Thus, in most cases, monochrome underpainting is retouched with colored glazes into which opaque colors can then be placed. Modeling is done during underpainting, but must shine through the layers of glaze. Painting with glazes is also used in making corrections.
Irrespective of which painting technique is chosen, one technical rule must in any case be observed, namely, that the lower layers must always be lean, and the fat layers (those containing more oil) must be on top. This also applies to the underpainting of a picture.
The following technical points should also be noted: the thicker the layers of color that are painted over one another, the greater is the possibility of cracking or even "bursting off" of the pigment. This is particularly true when using binding media that dry with a high degree of tension. It is, therefore, understandable that thin layers of color, applied as glazes, guarantee much better stability because of their very low state of tension. Glazing over in layers, nevertheless, has the disadvantage that the colors lose their luminosity and purity sooner and can easily result in a dingy effect.

Underpainting can be undertaken with both oil and tempera pigments. When using tempera pigments, an intermediate varnish is recommended, consisting of a thin dammar solution. In both cases underpainting should take place in such a way that it is incorporated in the final effect of the picture. Such preparatory work can, of course, be carried out in one or more colors.

Example of a painting carried out in layers,
which in the original shows an underpainting (ocher shade)

Methods of painting

The history of art provides apparently never-ending sequence of stylistic changes from all creative periods in the history of man. The application of color and manner of painting — we speak of the "technique" of a master — are basically an acknowledgment of the type of painting that is imagined by the painter and is proper to his nature as a creator of his own small world. We know that every person sees the world around him with different eyes. This is particularly so with artistically creative people. A decisive factor also is the variety of temperament expressed in the handling of a brush. We know, however, that man is subjected to certain changes in the course of his life, resulting from internal and external influences, that may transform his method of artistic expression. In the chapter on "The Painting of the Old Masters," reference has already been made to the method of painting of the aging Rembrandt; it is provacative and full of tension in his last self-portraits, in contrast to his earlier creations. Parallels would appear to exist here between the serious graphological judgment of handwriting and an investigation of the artist's brush-handling as revealed to the observant viewer in the work of a personality. In the case of a carefully executed painting in layers, the personal handwriting recedes behind the well-considered method of painting. Criteria such as composition, coloring, or the choice of subject can, here too, provide us with information about the artist's nature. **Alla prima** painting, however, gives us the possibility of following almost every brushstroke on the canvas.

Van Gogh very often discussed and wrote about technical and artistic matters. He tried to explain the nature of both his handling of the brush and his choice of colors, insofar as it was a question of basic concepts. Thus, for example, he wrote: "It is not the strong use of color that makes the painter. Yet, in order to make a soil quite vigorous, in order to shape the air clearly, we must not let it depend on a tube. Sometimes the subject itself determines whether we paint thinly, sometimes it is dictated by the material, the nature of things themselves, that the colors have to be applied thickly." And elsewhere he wrote: "I was struck by how powerfully the trunks are rooted in the soil; I began them with the brush, and I did not succeed in expressing the characteristic feature of the

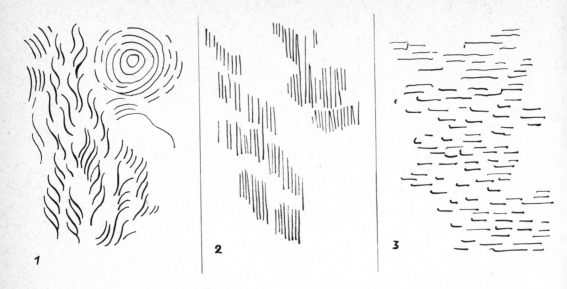

1. Van Gogh's handling of the brush. 2. The slanting layers of strokes used by Paul Cézanne
in many of his paintings. 3. Handling of the brush that resembles a brick wall.
The picture is composed of a juxtaposition of broad horizontal brushstrokes.
See also the illustration on page 80

soil which was already put on with thick colors; a stroke of the brush disappeared as nothing in it. I therefore pressed out roots and trunks from the tube and modelled them somewhat with the brush; they are now sticking in it, growing out from it and have taken root vigorously."

Concerning the use of colors, Van Gogh said: "No blue without yellow and without orange, and if you paint blue, do paint yellow and orange as well!" This is a direct reference to the use of complementary colors. The endeavor to represent a material as genuinely as possible with the help of color has sometimes led to adulteration with other substances. Thus, we know that Paula Modersohn at times mixed her pigments with fine sand, so that the sur — face of certain objects could be given a suitably individual form. (See also supplement plates IV and V)

The handle of the brush fulfilled a similar purpose in giving a different structure to a thickly applied colored surface. Other painters have mixed their pigments with sawdust and the like for the same reasons, or in place of a brush have used a spatula which gives a wide powerful oil-color technique. Even if a painter's application of color can alter according to the subject, nevertheless in many cases we find a preference for certain brush structures. With Cézanne, for example, the use of the slanting brushstroke is characteristic, allowing him even more gentle color chords than painting with a wide knife as he had

72

Example of a painting that shows both a round and straight brush technique.

Example of an **alla prima** painting that necessitates a brisk technique and a stronger application of color without any underpainting and final glazes. This type of painting is the most common today, both for nature studies and for large pictures

74

Oil painting in the form of a sketch,
which combines a brisk, almost watercolorlike treatment with a thicker application of color

Paula Modersohn-Becker, Portrait of an elderly lady.
The painting clearly shows a subsequent working up of the thick application of color

previously done. This is a type of drawing with the brush, as Cézanne said himself. The thousand brushstrokes of a picture, which have been set down side by side, combine ultimately in absolute harmony.

Van Gogh, who like Cézanne also considered the problem of pure color, followed the forms in his handling of the brush. Through his habit of bunching together and simplifying form, combined with his cultivated world of color, he achieved expressive and beautiful results.

The brushstroke is not only in a position to stress an external motion, it is also a means of expressing the personality itself. It does, of course, require a certain facility and practice before one's own "handwriting" can crystallize. In oil painting and tempera, there is a further factor of decisive importance, namely, the distance which the artist places between himself and his easel. Whether it be a landscape, still life, or portrait, the painter should never stand too near his canvas. Since all paintings are, in any case, viewed from a certain distance, this fact must be considered while working. Non-observance of this rule has already greatly disappointed many a beginner. The intended effect of a picture has appeared strange and discordant; moreover, the painting has essentially lost its power of expression. For only if, during painting, one stands back again and again from the painting surface and views the work from a few yards' distance, can it be judged. There need then be no fear of too petty a treatment of the subject. In watercolor work, such a large distance between the eye and the surface of the paper is not absolutely necessary, since there are certain limits in this technique as regards size. Nevertheless, here too, a suitable distance can be very useful.

Before beginning any painting, the subject selected should be observed for a time. Thus the picture can be studied so exactly that the painter's work will proceed more easily. Light and shadow sections are fixed, the eye tests the prospects of the colors and ascertains the composition of the forms. During such a study the picture is born in the painter's mind, even before the first brushstroke has been made. It is, therefore, just as much a question of the eye as of the practiced hand. In techniques of painting that provide for the use of absolutely opaque colors, the preliminary drawing of a subject must be restricted to the reproduction of the most essential outlines only. All important details must then be undertaken as a last part of the brush work.

It is very instructive from time to time to repeat the same subject for pictures. Progress can best be judged from such variations. It is always interesting to observe the change, that is, the improvement of color sensitivity in a succession of the same aspects of nature. Similar repetitions should be undertaken with still lifes and figure paintings. Apart from the study of colors, a further simplification of the shapes and movements will be observed. Experience has shown that such variants are always in the interests of improvement in painting.

Example of a painting in which an almost exclusively vertical handling of the brush predominates

78

Portrait which has been carried out entirely with a spatula technique

Paul Signac, Port de Mer. A picture which, by its technique, recalls a mosaic

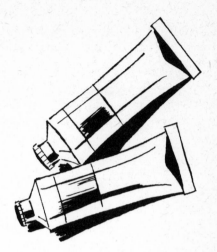

Oil Painting

The oil technique involves painting with viscous pigments that, as a binding medium, chiefly contain linseed oil or also poppy oil. If one prefers not to grind the individual pigments for oneself, after the example of the Old Masters and their workshops, one will, in most cases, resort to the handy tubes that are provided, ready for the palette, by the color industry. Most often a bristle brush will be used. The ground for painting can be canvas, wood, cardboard, plastic sheeting, or paper. This ground must be prepared for taking oil colors, to prevent rapid and excessive absorption.

Oil painting has occupied the main place among techniques of panel painting for about five hundred years. It allows a glazing and thick application of paint as well as the use of the palette knife. Initially one should be satisfied with a narrow and simple choice of colors. Only after sufficient mixing tests have been carried out with these colors, will one progress to extending and supplementing them. The table contained in this chapter shows the colors divided into three groups according to their applicability. It is not advisable to attempt to supplement the colors mentioned here by any other doubtful products. Such pigments are, in most cases, unsuitable for artistic purposes. They either darken too strongly or turn yellow to a marked extent. In addition, a large number of these pigments cannot be used for mixing purposes (chemical decomposition).

The pigments		
	1. Cremnitz white	4. Madder lake
	2. Cadmium yellow	5. Ultramarine blue
	3. Cadmium red	6. Prussian blue or Paris blue

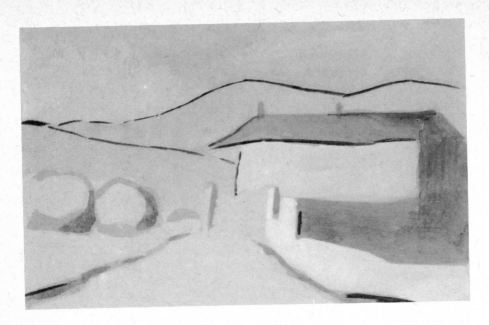

The plan for an oil painting excludes all details.
The essential features of the subject are first applied to the ground, using broad brushstrokes

This is followed by further additions that are also put in **alla prima**

The finished **alla prima** painting. Light and shadow sections round off the work

in any case suffice for giving a rich range of color by mixing. Green shades, from the brightest fresh green to heavy blue-green, are obtained by mixing Prussian blue and cadmium yellow. By a suitable addition of cadmium red, a duller and warmer green mixture is obtained.

Since the flexibility of tube colors does not always meet expectations and since the choice of the ground for painting has a decisive influence, the pigments must be prepared on the palette. For this, a painting medium is used that gives the pigment a certain flexibility and can be mixed personally.

It consists of $^1/_3$ dammar solution

$^1/_3$ unbleached linseed oil (no varnish)

and $^1/_3$ French turpentine.

Turpentine has a tendency to evaporate rapidly. A large amount of it can, of course, accelerate the drying process, but there is a danger of the pigments scaling off, if the dammar and linseed oil content in the tube color is not adequate.

The setting up of the palette is more or less an individual matter, but one should at an early stage get used to a certain order in the succession of colors. It has proved useful to begin at the left side of the palette with the white colors. These are followed by the yellows, reds, and blues, the dark pigments being on the right. Above and below this arrangement, there is then room for the green and/or brown shades. Eventually, the artist will know his way about his palette as well as the musician knows his instrument.

The painting itself should not be begun with too small a brush, for initially it is a matter of obtaining smooth execution. Oil colors have covering properties, so that details need not be present in the plan for painting.

Sketch and study

Much as the beginner's wish is directed towards a "finished" and completed picture, he must first of all come to terms with the material. For that reason the colored sketch and, in addition, the colored study form the first step on this path. It should be borne in mind that even trained painters, those who are well versed in the techniques of oil painting, again and again resort to preparing sketches and studies if they plan a largish painting. There is often confusion about the terms sketch and study. It should therefore be stressed that a sketch expresses the whole picture in a loose version, whereas a study requires a thorough treatment of some important parts of a picture. In the case of a portrait, for example, various detailed sketches will first be made, just as with figure compositions. Sketches and studies as aids may also be painted on strong paper that has previously been grounded with a thin solution of glue (size). The method of execution, in most cases characteristic of a sketch, should be carried over to the finished work.

Planning the picture

The planning of a picture begins with the area. Even if the forms are later to be stressed plastically, the juxtaposition of planes of color first dominates the painting ground. These color areas should, however, be separated from one another and should aim for a color contrast. The illustrations on pages 85 and 87 show that the final effect of contrast is already evident in the plan for the picture. A clear picture arises only from simplifying all the forms. The objects in the picture must have a sense of order resulting from the light and shadow sections. It is wrong if shadow areas are put in only with some dark dirty tones. All shadow sections must contain color if they are not to appear as dull and expressionless beside the colored light sections.

When planning a picture, care should be taken that the color areas are inserted with good contrasts

Painting in the open air

In contrast to studio painting, which was quite usual into the nineteenth century, deliberate painting in the open air, also called "pleinairism," admitted the colors of bright nonrefracted sunlight. This was a prerequisite for Impressionism, which was characterized by freshness and liveliness, compared with studio painting. Only in the midst of nature was the feeling for the finest and most varied color nuances aroused, and this, which painters worked out in the open air, was received favorably among artists, compared with pictures that up till then had been carried out indoors. Starting in France, this new form of painting gradually conquered the whole world in the last quarter of the nineteenth century. At the head of the new movement stood the painters who were among the most important in France, namely, Manet, Monet, Pissarro, Renoir, and so on. These were the first to capture on the canvas, rapidly and suffused with light, the lively expressive beauty of nature and humanity. This new movement had a marked effect everywhere.

Today this working in nature has become obvious, and painting in the open air is a general form of expression, alongside studio work (which in our time is dominated by abstract painting).

This is a "wet-in-wet painting," and in most cases is finished at one sitting surrounded by nature, unless it is a largish picture. The colors can be modulated as desired by painting them into one another. An effort must be made, however, to apply the colors immediately with a view to their ultimate effect. An underpainting may be used, in which further tonal values, such as light and shade, are applied immediately after the initial design, the final details being undertaken at the end. Or, as can be seen from the illustration on p. 90, each quarter inch of the scene from nature is placed on the ground in the finished state. This type of **alla prima** painting is like the piece-by-piece composition of a picture. In each case the next spot of color is dependent on the preceding brushstroke, if a harmonious and unified pictorial effect is to be achieved.

A decisive factor for the nature of a technique will, of course, be the subject itself, and the execution will be undertaken accordingly. It cannot be repeated often enough that in planning a picture all the unimportant things have to be removed. The subject has to be modified and, to a certain extent, also transformed and simplified. Only as a result of such simplification can the picture be made a strong expression of feeling.

If the easel is set up in front of an interesting subject that is worthy of being painted, and if the painter, filled with suspense, takes up his brush and palette,

Planning of a picture that contains much contrast.
The final effect can be recognized from the plan

then let it be said to all those who are untouched by the small act of creation which is now to ensue, that a minor or even major struggle is to begin between the painter and his subject. Only when the first signs of success are visible on the canvas, does the tension begin to abate, and the brushstrokes are applied with a greater degree of sureness. Wind and weather are not always favorable. A rising wall of cloud can change part of a landscape completely and render working difficult, or the sun may burn down mercilessly on the painter and his subject. Who will give up, however, despite flies or mosquitoes, if only an hour of intensive work is required? So begins the struggle with external circumstances, which will be forgotten completely if, after strenuous hours, the fresh and, we hope, successful open-air work is leaning against the studio wall, having been wrested in harmonious colors from nature.

Oil painting on a rough ground, requiring thick application of color

Still life

There was a time when a still life meant an accumulation of valuable showy vessels and luxurious foodstuffs. This was due less to the fact that in the sixteenth century the tables did possibly bend under the weight of selected game and rare fruits. Rather was it due to the view current at that time that a work of art, even a still life, should not contain any trivial objects. Later, in the Baroque era, this view remained unchanged. Noble wine in glasses and jugs and towering arrangements of flowers were placed on view and, on the canvas, kept a rendezvous with rare fish of the sea. Strangely enough, a draping made from the noblest velvet and expensive silk was also used. The buyer of such a still life wanted, for the price he paid, to see as many of these desirable articles in one picture as possible.

The painting of still lifes was led along different paths by Jean Baptiste Chardin

88

Landscape in **alla prima** painting, having the character of a sketch and painted in a short time from nature

(Paris, 1699–1779) who, in contrast to the previous overloaded and expensive-looking subjects, created the still life of the world of the ordinary citizen in honest and completely beautiful paintings. Here it was no longer a question of the appearance of affluence, but everyday objects were treated with artistic means to give entrancing compositions. Since then the still life has occupied a large place in the creation of many painters. It forms an essential part of the present and recent past in painting, and Van Gogh's sunflowers, like Cézanne's apples, compete with the fruit peelings of Gauguin and the tonally painted peasant crockery of Paula Modersohn.

The still life is, for the painter of today, again and again a test of artistic ability. Apart from the charm of color possessed by an earthenware jug, a glass, a herring, or fruit of any kind, the eternal problem of depth poses interesting

Alla prima painting in which one part of the picture has gradually been built on the other, as it were, without any uniform underpainting

questions. We have today become accustomed to seeing simple and unpretentious objects in still lifes, for which pictorial interpretation is the sole measure of value.

Portraits

By these we mean, in general, a representation of the human head, together with a complete or partial representation of the body. This requires in the first place a reproduction of the face taken from life. Such portraits have often been idealized. Portrait painting has, however, in the course of time grown away from the reproduction of the external appearance. People have rightly also demanded to see the inner features and temperament of the person portrayed, so that the complete portrait should show the person's whole appearance and nature. This requires a working out of the subject's most typical features. Skill in drawing forms the basis for this, since without it portrait and figure painting cannot even begin. This does not mean that there is no need for drawing skill in a landscape or still life. In these fields only by diligence and perseverance can a skillful preliminary drawing be made, while in the case of a portrait and figure, the certain mastery of drawing is absolutely indispensable. The layman can also very quickly recognize incorrect drawing and other errors. In portrait painting we must, therefore, not only lay down the usual outline, but must draw throughout the whole work with the brush, from the first to the last stroke. Any points that are not clean must be completely removed with the spatula; overpainting only results in "tortured" spots which, in the total picture, resemble dirty marks. Experience teaches that a white ground is not advisable. Toned grounds have always proved best for portrait painters, facilitating the placement of the colors, particularly for the beginner. Today an effort is made to paint a portrait as smoothly as possible in one or two sittings, for in portraits there should also be an attempt to extract the best in fresh **alla prima** painting, by beginning with the medium tones and then inserting the depths necessary for the plastic appearance. One should be sparing in the use of lights, these being applied lost. (See supplement plate VI).

Carl Hofer, Composition.
This is not a naturalistic tracing, but represents maximum simplification of the forms and movement

Carl Hofer, Wine-drinker.
A painting which resulted in a compact and, at the same time, dynamic effect by working out the essential features

Carl Hofer, Composition

Essential Pigments	Supplementary Pigments	Unsuitable Pigments
Zinc white	Cremnitz white	Zinc yellow
	Lithopone	Chromium yellow
	Titian white	
Cadmium yellow, bright	Naples yellow	Umber
	Ocher, burnt	Cassel brown
	Terra Pozzuoli	
Ocher, bright	English red	van Dyck brown
	Caput mortuum	
	Venice red	Vermilion
Sienna, burnt	Permanent red	Saturn red
	Fast red	
Cadmium red, bright	Cobalt violet, dark	Carmine
	Ultramarine blue	Madder pink
	Cobalt blue	
Alizarin madder lake	Cerulean blue	Cobalt violet, bright
	Chromium oxide green	Schweinfurt green
	Chromium oxide green, brilliant	
Paris blue (Prussian blue)	Green earth	English covering green
	Ivory black	Asphaltum
	Solid black	

Table of essential pigments, supplementary pigments that may be used, and pigments that are unsuitable for oil painting

Monochrome Painting (Grisaille Technique)

Just as the eye has become used to seeing a good photographic black-and-white reproduction as "colored," monochrome painting provides us in the same fashion with an absolutely convincing picture of the world around us. The possibilities in this watercolor technique are virtually unlimited. In practice, the colors used contain the whole scale from an extremely delicate tone to the most powerful depth. For this reason, brown (sepia) or gray colors (indigo) are preferred. India ink is also very suitable for grisaille technique. Apart from landscapes, monochrome painting can be used for all representations of figures, as well as for many applied art sketches. Sculptors prefer this technique, since it is possible in a few strokes of the brush to represent a comprehensive plastic form of expression. This art has been developed to a high degree of mastery in Japan and China, the hand in these countries having been suitably trained by writing exclusively with a brush. Without any preliminary drawing, pictures of plants, people, and animals are done with an elastic brushstroke. Grisaille technique should not be underestimated as a preliminary stage for real painting. Depending on the choice of paper structure, quite varying effects can be obtained. It is also possible to achieve

Josef Hegenbarth, Grisaille drawing

most delicate and powerful lines of extreme clarity as well as the finest gradations of tone on quite a rough ground.

In contrast to oil painting, in which, if possible, we first strike at the deepest and darkest chords, we adopt the opposite order in grisaille technique. The subjects are planned in large areas in delicate glazes, leaving the brightest effects blank. Then comes the next darkest plan and, in this way, the various tonal values up to the greatest depths are gradually worked out. An effort must be made to express the pictorial charm of the subject in such a manner that

Illustrative monochrome drawing

there are no hard and ugly edges. Care should, therefore, be taken that the color is always applied lightly and fluidly, so that when the work is complete, it does not, as the expert says, appear wooden. All grisaille trials serve at the same time as a preliminary stage for watercolor painting which, in common with grisaille technique, requires a fluid and smooth treatment with the brush. In practice, also carried out in one color are all those works intended as the original copy for reproductions and which require blending of the color tone. This includes monochrome reproductions of fashion drawings, illustrations, and so forth. In many cases such a copy is made, depending on the subject

98

Illustrative monochrome drawings

Monochrome watercolor painting with light areas left blank

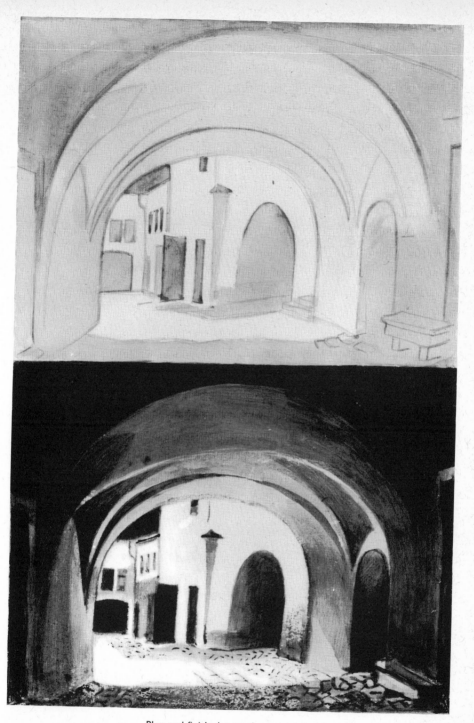

Plan and finished monochrome painting

Capri
1953

102

Grisaille brush drawing

and purpose, with tempera pigments (opaque pigments), the mixed technique of glazing and opaque pigments also being used for this.

Grisaille technique likewise serves for preliminary studies for graphic and painting work. There are innumerable grisaille drawings of this type by Rembrandt, which were used as basic preliminary studies for pictures and etchings. There are numerous works in this technique by Gavarni and Daumier, the famous French caricaturists and painters.

Apart from grisaille technique which, in common with watercolor, obtains the varying gradations by thinning the color or ink, there is also "dry brush" technique, in which all gradations of tone are achieved by light or heavier pressure of the brush. The flexibility of the brush not only allows a full deep-black surface, but the dry brush also gives particularly fine blendings that resemble those obtained by a wide stroke with chalk (see p. 104). It is necessary, however, that the brush should always contain only as much color or ink as is required to make a blend possible. By way of a test, the brush should first be stroked out on a piece of paper until the suitable degree of moisture is

103

Experiments with a dry brush

reached. The drawings made with a dry brush should not be too small, since then the artist cannot achieve the desired blendings. There will, no doubt, be one or another sketch in one's folio that can be worked over in this way.

Tempera Painting (temperare = to blend)

Painting in tempera technique can be traced back to the very beginnings of the arts. It can, therefore, be called the oldest painting process. In the course of time this technique has undergone many changes. It is known that the Babylonians and Assyrians already had a complete scale of colors; white, orange, purple, blue, red, black, green, and yellow occur in their paintings.

By tempera we mean a mixture of water-soluble pigment elements with a non-water-soluble binding medium. This medium may vary in origin, and in each case it lends its name to the tempera technique. Original tempera painting used pigments whose binding agent consisted mainly of egg yolk. We therefore speak of the egg tempera technique.

Egg tempera

A perfectly natural emulsion is formed if egg yolk and egg white are shaken together and diluted with water or size as desired. The hen's egg (yolk) contains a percentage of oil, called egg oil. This is a yellowish oil that becomes viscous, but does not belong to the class of real drying oils or siccatives. It is distributed in the yolk in the form of extremely small droplets, thus preventing it from separating out. There is no separation even on diluting the egg yolk with water. A milky liquid is formed that, even when stored for prolonged periods, does not experience any oil separation. Egg tempera resembles oil pigment most closely in its optical effect. It is, however, a technique in which we can speak of half oil and half watercolors. This has the advantage that, on drying, the colors lose less of their strength than in other watercolor techniques.

On the other hand, egg emulsions do not keep fresh for long. This is under-standable since the chemical constituents of the hen's egg contain sulfur, which on decomposing is liberated as hydrogen sulfide. Egg emulsions should, of course, only be prepared from fresh and perfect eggs. A drop of oil of cloves can improve the stability of the egg binder. It is always wise to prepare only a small amount (from one egg), since if it is used quickly, there is no danger of it being spoiled.

This easily prepared egg emulsion (yolk + white) had already been used as a binding agent for pigments in ancient times, and does not itself require any addition of resins or oils. Egg tempera ground in this way does not, however, allow any thick application of pigment.

The yolk, with about thirty percent oil content, can also be worked up into an emulsion (shaking and grinding, with a small addition of water or size).

The chemical composition of the hen's egg

	Yolk	White
Water content	51.5%	84.8%
Albumen (white of egg)	15.0%	12.0%
Oil content	30.0%	0.5%
Ash	1.4%	1.2%
Other constituents	2.1%	1.5%
	100.0%	100.0%

Egg tempera can likewise be used as an underpainting for oil colors, in the same way that an oil color ground can be overpainted with tempera pigments. In order to make possible the overpainting with tempera pigments on a fatty ground, commercial **purified ox gall** is used. It has the property of making fat to a certain extent compatible with water.

An egg tempera painting dries with a half gloss. This can be increased to a certain extent by "polishing" the well dried painting with a soft brush or soft rag. A coating of mastic varnish also gives the same gloss as shown by a var-nished oil painting.

106

Plan for a tempera painting on the basis of planes

Glue tempera

As the name implies, solutions of glue are used as the binding media in this tempera technique. In practice this technique is used today mainly for painting larger surfaces (decorations, fair stands, scenery painting).

Glue, as an animal product, is one of those substances which tend to become putrid. Thus the glue tempera technique will in the first place be used only for "short-lived" paintings. Glue tempera colors that have greater stability and a more flexible substance are obtained by the addition of linseed varnish. Since normally an emulsion of glue water and oil is not possible, alum is added. Linseed varnish can be mixed without difficulty into the viscous paste made from alum glue water and powdered pigment.

Bright types of glue have proved best in glue tempera painting. A glue solution in the ratio 50:1000 has proved successful by experience. The purest and also most colorless type of glue is gelatine which can be bought everywhere, being most often supplied in the form of thin sheets. Other glue substances, such as bone glue or glue from leather waste, which merely swell up in cold water, dissolve properly in hot water only. Even with a high degree of dilution, such solutions turn into a gel on cooling. It is, therefore, recommended that the glue colors be kept warm while working.

Oil tempera

Here proportional parts of oil and resin are added to an emulsion. According to their amount, they change the character of pure tempera painting to such an extent that the pigments cannot be processed with water. Oil of turpentine then serves as the painting medium. In reverse, of course, an oil pigment can be changed by the addition of water-soluble emulsion tempera so that an oil tempera is formed. This transformation is possible both with egg yolk emulsion and with undiluted casein emulsion. In any case, the native gloss is removed with the oil color. We say that is has been rendered "lean," thus leading to dull and flat colors.

The origin of present-day oil color is ascribed to the van Eyck brothers, who mixed oils and resins into an emulsion. We know with certainty only that the van Eyck brothers used an emulsion pigment whose composition has remained a secret up till now, in spite of intensive experiments.

The painting ground for tempera

The choice of ground for tempera painting is by no means as difficult as in other painting techniques. There is practically no material to which these colors do not adhere. For types of tempera in which the colors are to be processed in a highly fluid state, that is, with a fairly high water content, a somewhat absorbent ground is used, while oil tempera and casein tempera can be applied to an almost smooth nonabsorbent ground. Apart from a white ground, which naturally stresses the brilliance of the pigments, colored grounds are also used in tempera painting techniques. Particularly when it is a question of tonal, shaded painting, gray, brown, or red grounds are preferable to a white painting surface. The material of the ground may be plywood or fiber board. Pasteboard is also suitable for smaller paintings, although it must not be too thin because of the possible danger of warping. In this case, a weak grounding with glue water (on both sides) is recommended. In the case of a tempera pigment that is soluble in water, a strong paper (watercolor paper or the like) may be used as the ground, so that too marked an absorption of color is avoided. The fact that all tempera techniques can also be used for painting on walls will be evident from the section on mural painting, in which **casein painting** is also discussed.

108

Gradations and blendings in tempera technique

Painting equipment for tempera

A tin-plate palette (with depressions) whose size is proportionate to the size of the pictures to be painted, with palette cups for emulsifiers, together with a series of ordinary watercolor and bristle brushes, forms the painting equipment. The choice of brushes will depend on the nature of the work and its size. The colors cannot be kept fresh by adding water, since then the binding medium contained in the pigment is weakened enormously. It is better to keep the palette in a cool place and wrap it in a moist cloth.

Choice of pigments for tempera painting

The most important pigments	Supplementary pigments	
Cadmium yellow, bright	Ivory black	
Light ocher	Umber, bright	
Cadmium red, bright	English red	
Alizarin madder lake		
Burnt Sienna	Chromium yellow	These can be used
Prussian blue	Chromium orange	with no fears in
Cobalt blue	Zinc yellow	tempera painting,
Cerulean blue	Sienna, nat.	but NOT in oil
Ultramarine blue	Umber, nat.	painting
Chromium oxide green		

Varnishing of tempera works

As in other painting techniques, varnishing of the pictures is also possible in tempera. Paintings that embodied this technique six hundred years ago were provided with a final coat of varnish that at first sight suggests a painting in oils. Rapid-drying varnishes for tempera painting are obtained by dissolving mastic and dammar resins in pure alcohol. These alcohol varnishes are, however, inferior to turpentine oil varnishes because of a certain degree of brittleness.

Decorative painting with tempera pigments

112

Tempera painting on canvas in which the structure of the ground can be seen

Alcohol varnishes take only a short time to dry and are popular for works in which decomposition of the painting may result from turpentine; nevertheless, greater suppleness is obtained with oil of turpentine varnish.

Should an intermediate varnish be used before the work is complete, then a weak dammar solution suffices for this. For the final coat, it is better to work with several thin solutions. Even if the first and second coats peel off and the colors initially become darker, but remain dull, the desired full gloss will result in the course of a few days. In this case, too, each coat must dry, sometimes for hours, before we can think of a further coat of varnish. For applying varnishes, an approximately six centimeters wide soft bristle brush is used, with which the coat is applied in uniform strokes. Nitrocellulose lacquers (zapon varnishes) are also suitable for the preliminary varnishing of a picture. They form a rapid insulation, but give only a low degree of gloss.

Another type of final varnish is beeswax paste, which is applied thinly in circular movements with a pad of cotton wool. After this paste has dried thoroughly, the layer is worked on with a soft brush until a dull silklike gloss has developed.

Designing

For a preliminary drawing for tempera technique, a soft pencil is suitable, as is also chalk or charcoal. Practiced hands will, depending on the difficulty of the subject, undertake a preliminary drawing immediately with the brush. It must, however, be remembered that the techniques discussed here use opaque pigments. Tempera pigments may also, of course, be used as glazes, but the proper preparation is aimed at the covering power of the colors. What has been said elsewhere, in the section on oil painting, regarding the preliminary drawing, thus also applies to tempera painting.

Preservation of tempera works

If framing under glass is not envisaged, tempera works must be kept flat, that is, in an unrolled state. When framed, care should definitely be taken that a suitable distance is preserved between the surface of the picture and the glass. Moisture penetrates everywhere and then causes unpleasant spots to form on the glass.

Watercolor and Gouache Painting

The name of this painting technique is derived from the Latin word "aqua," meaning water. It is, therefore, a painting process in which the colors are merely stirred with water and diluted. The coating of pigment can, even after years, again be made soluble through the action of water, unless a special fixative is applied after completion of the painting.

The binding media for pure watercolor painting consist of gum arabic and honey. The use of opaque colors is excluded, if the special character of watercolor is to be preserved. The brightness of the ground, whether it be paper, parchment, or any other, makes possible the omission of highlights, which should not, therefore, be obtained by any white pigments. If these requirements are not fulfilled, the freshness that must specially characterize watercolor is jeopardized from the start. It follows from this that the very first brushstrokes determine through their tonal value the nature of the whole color scale of a watercolor. Watercolor painting is painting with light and should preserve the transparency and purity of the colors. Too substantial, or too thickly applied, sections of color will only reduce the impression of a light and airy character. "Dirty" areas will occur, which can only rarely be corrected later. Watercolor has been called a painting of accidental effects. All the same, these "accidental effects" must be mastered. Dryness of the brush and heaviness of the pigments stand in crass contrast to water, to the fluidity of the material which the watercolor requires. Effects of depth, such as are achieved with oil pigments, should not be attempted with watercolors. This technique is also not suitable for larger works; it can, however, be used for colored impressions to a greater extent than almost any other technique used in painting.

Painting with watercolors can, from a historical point of view, be equated with the beginnings of painting itself. As with every type of painting, watercolor has in the course of time been subjected to various changes in use and conception of technique, quite apart from the personal "handwriting" of the artist.

Thus, for example, a start was made in England, which has always been a special center for watercolors, with a correct underpainting of the subject in gray tone, this then becoming the support for the sparingly glazed color gradations (eighteenth century). The painter M. W. Turner (1775–1831) is in this respect a famous exception. In his, colorful and shining watercolors he painted the landscapes of his English home in bold impressions. Turner used all the possibilities of absolute watercolor painting.

Later, in the nineteenth century, it was long the fashion to use only one shade of color and to interpret watercolor technique in sepia, indigo, or gray gradations only (see Monochrome Painting).

The ground for painting

In most cases, a white paper will be used for watercolor painting, the grain (smooth to rough) being a matter of preference. It must be realized that the detail of work in this technique depends on the degree of grain of the paper. A good watercolor paper contains linen fibers instead of wood and straw. Sizing should be carried out with animal glue. These papers are available today in a wide variety of thickness and sizes, naturally bleached (no bleaching powder solution!). It is impossible to recommend a given type, since a particular paper is required for every technique in watercolor painting. Emil Nolde (1867–1956), for example, preferred to use India papers of varying coloration for his colorful watercolors, while others prefer Ingres paper.

Paintings on fabric or board are exceptions. When painting on fabric, gouache pigment is used, just as when painting on colored paper.

The technique

It can be said that there is no other field of painting which offers such a multitude of methods of expression as watercolor. This technique makes it possible to enter very exactly into the smallest and finest details, even as with the same pigments a large-scale, decorative, even heavy color impression can be obtained. This ability to vary the expression has undoubtedly helped watercolor

116

Water determines the character of watercolor painting. The same tone superimposed after drying in each case gives a more intensive coloring

painting to become extremely popular. For this reason people have also given up the completely erroneous view that watercolor is a second-class art that should be subordinated to oil painting. The value of a work can never depend on the cost of the materials used, but should rest exclusively on the result which confronts us. It is not the means that are the determining factor, but what is achieved by the most varied means.

Painting in watercolors begins with the application of uniform washes of color for purposes of technical drawing. The architect uses watercolor in order to plan his sketches in color; the commercial artist works with the same materials, as do the fashion artist and the designer of industrial products. In all these works the line is the boundary of the area of color. It is, therefore, initially a question of drawings planned in color in which the color is a supporting factor. Alongside these is the pure watercolor, in which the line plays a subordinate role to the color that dominates the picture.

For all areas that have to be planned, the suitable amount of pigment must be ground with water in small glass or porcelain cups. Only in this way can spotless designs be obtained. The pure watercolor does not require this aid for artistic expression. The small enamel palette in the watercolor box suffices for the painter to mix his shades, which should then be applied to the paper in a rapid manner with a marten-hair brush

The equipment for watercolor painting is not extensive. Apart from the watercolor block or drawing-board, with paper stretched over it, and the box of watercolors, a selection of marten-hair brushes (round brushes, sizes 4–10), and a container for water are required. A piece of linen for wiping the brushes and a piece of natural sponge for brightening areas of color that have become too dark complete the equipment.

The brushes should not stand in the water container too long, since they can become misshapen as a result. Care should always be taken that brushes are not kept in too small a color box. Once the tip of the brush has been deformed, in most cases, it cannot be restored to its original shape.

Colors

A watercolor box with a thumbhole and containing either twelve or fourteen colors has proved very successful. In practice, the following selection will always prove adequate, the use of the handy bricks or tubes being purely a personal matter.

> **Cadmium yellow, bright**
> **Cadmium orange**
> **Ocher, bright**
> **Madder lake**
> **Cadmium red**
> **English red**
> **Caput mortuum**
> **Cobalt blue**
> **Ultramarine blue**
> **Prussian blue (Paris blue)**
> **Chromium oxide green, brillant**
> **Green earth**
> **Terra di Sienna, burnt**
> **Umber**
> **Payne's grey**

The preliminary drawing

There is a wide variety of possibilities for this, depending on the sureness of the artist, the subject chosen, and the size of the watercolor. The intended artistic expression will also determine the nature of the preliminary drawing. An architectural work that enters into details requires a clear but rapid outline drawing. If this has been carried out too inexactly and indistinctly, it definitely makes it difficult to apply the colors with certainty.

If the preliminary drawing is made with charcoal instead of with a pencil (for larger sizes), the charcoal should be dusted off with a piece of rag before beginning to paint. Charcoal has the property – as have also very soft types of pencils – of dissolving in combination with water, so that impurity of the colors can result.

Skilled watercolor artists sometimes begin without any preliminary drawing or do this straightaway with the brush, using a neutral shade. In general, the preliminary drawing should be restricted to the main outline form. If this is correct, then the artist can concentrate on the application of color, necessary details of drawing being a matter for the brush.

The design itself can determine the nature of the finished work.
Watercolor offers all possibilities of expression

The rapid and powerful quality of the plan for a watercolor in which the outlines are particularly stressed and determine the expression of the picture

Watercolor in which the final effect has been obtained by superimposed painting in layers

Gouache painting

This is a type of watercolor painting. The linguistically correct term for this painting technique is "guazzo," meaning "watercolor." The difference between watercolor painting and gouache technique consists primarily in that watercolors are applied as a glaze, so that the ground shines through the colors and in this way helps to determine the effect of the picture, while in gouache painting the ground does not appear. This is achieved by mixing a highly opaque pigment with watercolor. The essential feature is that the opaque pigment is worked wet-in-wet, resulting in a fine and harmonious union of color. Both types of painting, watercolor and gouache, can also be used together. This is called "half-gouache painting." Apart from use in free painting, this technique is also used in the applied arts.

122

Gouache painting on light-colored tinted paper

Watercolor in which only the picturesque expression is emphasized

124

In architectural studies the picturesque element can also predominate over the strictly linear conception

125

Martin Koblo, Landscape, watercolor

Martin Koblo, Landscape, watercolor

Example of a watercolor that shows marked contrasts and extremely powerful painting

128

Painting with Colored Pencils

People like to reach for a colored pencil if circumstances make a rapid and non-time-consuming recording of a colored subject necessary. This technique, with its open crayons or those enclosed in wood, does not involve a material that perhaps may not satisfy higher artistic demands. There is no such technique, for the decisive point is the ability to recreate what is seen in an artistic manner with the materials available. When using colored pencils (we are not discussing pure pastel crayons here), we shall of course, have to do without the finest intermediate tones, but transitions of tone are quite possible by superimposing strokes of color. The juxtaposition of points and strokes of color can also provide charming color effects, as seen in the paintings of the French artists Monet, Pissarro, or Signac.

Colored pencils and chalks can also serve as useful materials for preliminary studies. It is best to avoid an ordinary pencil for preliminary drawings, since colored pencils contain a foreign body that is technically incompatible with it. It is more correct, if a preliminary drawing is required, to do this with a colored pencil. The use of white paper will show up the luminosity of colored pencils at their best, but picturesque effects can also be obtained with such pencils on colored to black paper or cardboard ground.

Since this technique is one in which the line predominates as the means of expression – in contrast to painting – these lines dominate the picture, and continue so until its completion.

There is little to be said about the method of working itself. The handling is similar to that of any other drawing pencil, except that it is the color which has to speak. When sketching landscapes, an effort should be made, as in other techniques, to simplify the form and color. Painting with colored pencils is not, however, solely a technique that need be restricted to the sketch book. Advertising art in its manifold aspects makes use of colored pencils. The designer uses them partly or entirely for posters, packages, illustrations, booklets, and book covers, and can in this way confer charming effects of color on his works. Examples of this are found in the colorful drawings and posters by the French artist Henri de Toulouse-Lautrec (1864–1901), whose colored pencil drawings often remind us of beautifully colored Japanese woodcuts. (See also supplement plates VII and VIII)

Colored pencils can, in combination with watercolor or tempera painting, appropriately enliven both these techniques. It is technically possible to work over a watercolored surface with a colored pencil, but in tempera technique the pencil remains an independent element within the painting. The two very different techniques can, nevertheless, be combined harmoniously.

M. Koslo
1945   Worpswede

Colored pencil drawing from nature in which the juxtaposition of strokes results in a unity of color

Colored Drawings

In all the techniques described so far, it has been a question of artistically creative merit and independent construction. It is different if an outline drawing made with black ink, using a brush or pen, is to be colored. Particularly luminous colored inks are primarily used for this. These inks have glazing properties, and thereby preserve their purity over the white of the ground. They should be diluted with distilled water. Since these pigments are non-water-soluble after drying, we must be clear about the fields of color to be filled in before beginning work. In order to obtain uniformly colored areas, the fields to be painted can be laid in lightly with distilled water before the actual application of color. Black ink should not be used if mixtures of colors with these inks should be necessary. Coloring should preserve the purity of the pigment, and this is prejudiced by mixing with black. Watercolors are, of course, also suitable for these purposes.

Colored drawings are used in advertising art and can also form part of an architectural outline or plan. This technique is also used in certain cases to color graphic work, such as illustrations for smaller or special editions of books. This form of decoration has been taken over from older times, such as, for example, when monochrome woodcuts or copper engravings were worked over with watercolors. This is a custom that has extended down to the present day, when multicolor printing cannot be used with very small editions, possibly for reasons of economy. Works that are sometimes colored also include small examples of graphic art for special occasions, such as Ex Libris plates, notices of a private nature, records, diplomas, and so forth. Finally, in this category are all sketches concerned with the color designing of rooms. It is much easier and, in any case, safer to make a small-scale design before planning the color of particular rooms than to make tests on the spot, which even then may not prove satisfactory. The same applies to the color designing of stands at fairs and similar exhibition buildings.

132

Painting with Pastels

This technique is possibly more suitable than any other for capturing momentary moods in nature. For this reason, it is often rightly used as a preliminary stage for oil painting. Working with soft and versatile pastels is to be recommended for studies of any type. Compared with other painting techniques, pastel painting is wrongly considered to be a method of expression for use by amateurs. Nothing is more incorrect than this view. What is really the case is that the unpracticed hand and certainly also the untalented one are confused by the rich choice of shades offered by a box of pastels. Pastel technique suffers from a slight disadvantage owing to the sensitivity of the pigments. Damage easily occurs from pressure and unskilled treatment of the sheets. Quite unintended changes must also be expected when fixing, unless tests have been carried out in this direction.

Pastel pigments are made in two degrees of hardness, and they should not be used together. It is better to use only the soft type, since otherwise, besides scratching the ground, the soft character of pastel is lost. Among all pastel colors there are about a hundred shades that can be used. All other tone gradations form an unnecessary and excessive encumbrance. As in oil painting, there is among the several hundred pastel colors a large number of shades with which care is needed. These are principally the aniline pigments which are either not fast to light or, as a result of their intensity, penetrate through other colors. This penetration sometimes extends through all the superimposed layers of color.

The most important and suitable shades in pastel painting are the basic or full shades. All other twelve degrees of mixing are prepared from them. The basic shade has the designation G. The darkest mixed shade is designated by the letter A; the brightest degree of mixing from the full shade is designated by the letter O. Since the differences in tone between individual degrees of mixing

133

Pastel sketch on colored tinted paper. There are no decidedly blurred tones

134

are very slight, it suffices when buying pastels to make a selection that omits every second shade. From the basic shade, for example, the order would be A · C · E · G · I · L · N. The color scale should be restricted as far as possible, since it is difficult to differentiate between too many color nuances. It is quite adequate if, apart from the full shades, there are about five or six mixed grades made from them. Since each pastel color can be bought separately, a selection may be made according to personal inclinations and intentions.

The dry pigments used in pastels have no possibility of yellowing or subsequently darkening. The freshness of color is, therefore, preserved for long periods, particularly if the pastel painting has been placed under glass. A further advantage is that when working in the open air there is no drying process to be waited for.

As in oil painting where the palette is "set up" differently for a portrait or a landscape, there is in pastel painting a difference between a selection of chalks mainly suitable for a portrait and one which is suitable mainly for landscapes. Such a standard selection can, of course, be extended and modified as required. The subject chosen and also the personal color sensitivity of the artist decide in each case. It is more important, first of all, that shades which are fast to light be used.

The ground

A specially prepared paper in a wide variety of shades is available for pastel painting. These are velvetlike roughened papers that make working difficult for the beginner. Colored papers no doubt have a special charm, but it is here the same as with colored grounds for oil painting. A white ground does reproduce the colors in their greatest purity and transparency. Ingres or Titian papers (white or yellowish) are very suitable for pastel painting. If one has a special preference for a rougher ground (coarser granulation), then the paper or cardboard can be coated with ordinary starch paste. Powdered gypsum or pumice is then scattered carefully onto the still damp surface, superfluous powder being shaken off gently. Apart from paper, fine natural linen is also a suitable ground for pastel painting.

The technique

Pastel technique and the results of pastel painting are more versatile than is generally assumed. A work carried out with these chalks does not necessarily have to produce only soft and gently sweet effects, such as occur in many

135

portraits of women and children. The material is, in fact, so adaptable that it offers possibilities for every type of personal expression. In the hands of artists such as the Impressionists Degas, Pissarro, or Liebermann, and also as a tool for the Expressionists, these small sticks of chalk have proved eminently successful. (See also supplement plate IX)

The pastel drawing differs from the real **pastel painting** through its technical execution. While in the pastel drawing the effect of the ground has, as in every other drawing, to be taken into account, the painting requires a working over of the individual layers of color. The ground serves here only as a support for the color. It is, however, apart from the structure of the painting surface, of no importance for the final effect of the pastel painting. The picture surface is covered, as in oil painting.

The color shades may be placed side by side in strokes and the ground left as in any other drawing; or else the pastel layer may be wiped or blurred, in order to obtain uncommonly delicate gradations in color and tonal value. A master of pastel work was the Frenchman Degas (1834–1917), who combined both these techniques in his sometimes very large pastels. A deciding factor in the use of one or other type is, of course, the subject. The nature of the ground also plays a part, and naturally must be taken into account from the start in estimating the total effect of the pastel work.

It is absolutely necessary before actually beginning work with pastel colors that a few preliminary studies be carried out with the material. Since the pastel box is at the same time the palette, one should from the start get used to maintaining the order sticks exactly. Only thus can work be facilitated, since the exact position of the sticks should be imprinted on the painter's mind in the same way as the order of colors on a palette. Pastel colors are already mixed; fine and very fine color gradations can then be undertaken directly on the ground while painting, in contrast to other techniques.

The preliminary drawing for a pastel can be made with charcoal, but in such a case the outline drawing must be fixed. Experienced artists will, however, begin straightaway with the pastel stick itself. A colored underpainting with watercolor or opaque colors as a ground is not recommended at all. These two techniques are not only foreign to one another, but also pastel chalks cannot bind correctly with the ground. A final fixing of the painting does very little to alter this situation.

For larger works in pastels one should first begin with a sketch in a smaller format. Carrying out the real pastel drawing or painting is made very much easier by this method, since all the tonal values can be taken from the sketch. This procedure also saves unnecessary corrections, which mostly result in dirty areas.

136

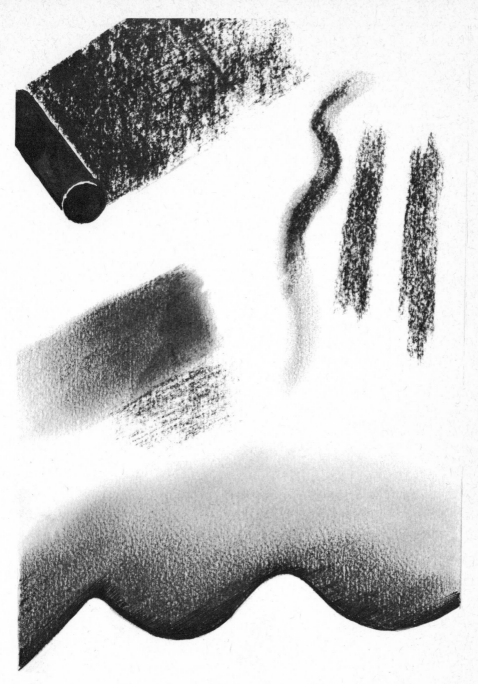

Tests with a stick of pastel.
The lower drawing shows the blending which can be obtained by using a stencil

137

Since all pastel sticks have good covering power, it suffices to plan the work in gentle tones. In contrast to watercolor painting, which is begun with the brightest shades, pastel work is planned in the medium tones, the most powerful color gradations then gradually being developed. The bright and light areas are inserted last. One should begin with simple still lifes, the areas of the subject being put in first. Only later, when the color and tone contrasts are present, are the other colors worked in giving the picture its real charm. A brown area, for example, may be enlivened by a red one, a blue area by green accents. As in painting, the main thing is that there should be an effort to achieve a unity of color and form.

The fixing of the pastel takes place with a special paste fixative that can be obtained everywhere. Since the pastel sticks do not contain any real binding medium, this has to be replaced by the fixative. It is possible to undertake individual intermediate fixings while working, so that for the final fixing only a light spraying of the drawing is needed. This has the advantage of preserving the character of the pastel better, since too pronounced a fixing can alter the colors considerably. In the case of paper which is not too strong, the pastel, like any other drawing, can be fixed by coating the back with a brush, without using the fixative tube. Fixing must also be tested on individual samples of pastels before a finished work is spoiled. A fixing solution can be prepared by dissolving two grams of white colophony powder in alcohol or pure benzine. Those who can afford to preserve finished pastels in the unfixed state by laying a sheet of cellophane between each of them will preserve the special charm of the technique. On the other hand, the sheets always remain sensitive as long as they are not framed behind glass.

The nature of this painting technique is really a combination of drawing and painting. The name "pastel" comes from the Italian "pasta," meaning "dough." The manufacture of the colored sticks takes place by mixing a white body with the finely pulverized pigment. Just enough binding agent is added to this mixture to transform it into a dough that is ready for use after drying.

Sketch for a portrait made with pastel chalks

Plan for a still life in pastels.
The bright and dark sections are put in first, further elaboration being carried out later

Colored Woodcuts

When the woodcut and linocut make use of color as a means of expression, these techniques leave the field of the graphic arts. By the addition of color they approach painting and can even become part thereof. Originally, the woodcut often appeared in a brightly colored form, since the black prints were colored by hand. The tendency towards color led to many experiments, which finally found fulfillment in the use of different plates. Thus, as early as the middle of the fifteenth century, a start was made with decorating books with printed initial letters in red or blue, unless this two-color effect was obtained by subsequent treatment of the pages with brush or pen.

Beginning in 1486 there appeared in Augsburg particularly decorative colored editions of books that show the use of various colors on one page. This juxtaposition of colored areas ceased at the beginning of the sixteenth century, and led to a plastic development of the woodcut, stressing the white effects caused by the cut-out areas.

Here a tinted plate of medium color strength (gray or brown) was used, into which all the light parts were worked, while a further plate reproduced the black drawing. This type of two-color woodcut is today just as common as in previous centuries. It was spread mainly by the prints of Hans Burgkmair (1473–1531), Lucas Cranach (1472–1553), Hans Baldung Grien (1476–1545) and Albrecht Altdorfer (1480–1538).

In Italy the colored woodcut developed on a broader plane than in Germany. The Italian use of several plates contrasted with the woodcut method practiced by such masters as Albrecht Dürer (1471–1528) and Hans Holbein (1470–1524), both of whom used merely individual tinted plates.

The colored woodcut led to quite different results in China and particularly in Japan, showing pictorial effects for more than in the European countries. Its influence has been of very great importance for the whole of European painting during the last eighty years. Here the otherwise strict and striking black-and-white technique of the woodcut developed through the use of color to a watercolorlike character, conditioned by the gentle blendings of color that are a feature of Chinese and Japanese prints. Watercolor was, in fact, used for printing these colored woodcuts, suitably diluted to obtain the desired effect. This accounts for that gentleness and transparency which we admire in Chinese and Japanese prints with their strong ties to people and landscapes.

Before one starts to make a colored woodcut, the difficulties inherent in the monochrome woodcut must first be overcome. As for the latter, a draft is required which should allow for the technical possibilities to a great extent and which is suitable for a woodcut through simplification of the drawing. A drawing study, irrespective of its type, must first be prepared, therefore, for transfer to the wood block or to the lino block, naturally taking into account the color effect.

Since a separate one has to be cut for each color, the color blocks will accordingly be restricted to only a few. Further gradations can, of course, be obtained by color overprinting, just as the various types of colored woodcut allow quite different and variable possibilities of expression. If one prefers not to make an outline block into which the individual color blocks can be built, as it were, charming effects can be obtained by using only colored areas which have in turn been partly worked with the knife. Basically, the colored woodcut cannot dispense with simplicity of line and area, if the character of the technique is to be preserved.

If all these difficulties cannot be coped with at once, it is better to begin with the two-block woodcut. The final effect of the cut can be determined beforehand if colored paper (tinted paper) is used when designing, so that the lights can be placed on it with a brush or pen. The paper thereby gives the effect of the tinted block.

In contrast to the monochrome woodcut, the multicolored variety requires special design equipment for purposes of matching. Only with this device and with exactly cut paper can a perfectly matched color print be obtained. The individual color blocks should also, of course, be aligned correspondingly, so that agreement is assured in the reverse transfer of the drawing onto the wooden block. Exactly applied tracings, conforming to the correctly shaped blocks, also facilitate the matching up of the color print.

For the actual printing process, pigments containing either varnish (printing inks) or watercolor can be used. The latter are commercially available, ready for use, as Japan aquacolors. Since the covering power of these pigments can vary considerably, either greater transparency may be obtained by adding a small amount of water, or the colors may be given stronger covering ability by adding white pigment.

142

The Japan aquacolor can be applied to the printing block with a short bristle brush, the color first being used as it comes from the tube. A soft camel-hair brush moistened with water then serves to distribute the color as desired. The more uniformly the printing pigment is distributed on the printing block, the more uniform will be the printed colored surface. The most suitable degree of fluidity of the pigment will be discovered after a few tests. In no case should one work with too thin a pigment, since the paper, which is moistened before printing, then acquires too great an absorptive power, resulting in unclean prints.

Supple and flexible India paper is best used for printing. The sheet, cut to the correct size, is moistened with a clean wide camel-hair brush and is placed

between gently absorptive waste sheets. Prepared for printing in this way, the sheet is allowed to stand for about an hour under slight pressure, so that uniform distribution of the liquid can take place. Printing with watercolors requires a greater degree of skill, compared with the use of printing inks (varnish colors). More charmingly colored prints can, however, be obtained by this method.

The color application, when using printing inks, takes place by means of a roller, and a print from the wooden block can also be made by using a wide and heavy roller. A further possibility of obtaining a good print is to use the burnisher. In the case of a particularly thin paper, a stronger and smooth sheet must be laid over it before the print can be made with the roll or burnisher. Since in our colored woodcuts it is solely a question of hand prints, an absorptive paper will always be preferred. The paper should be weakly sized. It must be able to adhere firmly to the inked printing block, so that no slipping is possible during the printing process. It may also be expected that a good printing paper will have a certain degree of strength. If for some reason a pure white paper is not chosen, the correct paper can be chosen from the wide selection of long-fibered India papers that do not tear easily. These papers, with their yellowish or slightly brownish tint, reduce the sometimes quite powerful coloring and ensure a harmonious total effect.

We should like to refer once again to the undisputed masters of the colored woodcut, namely the Japanese and Chinese. Their unique works in this field express the perfection of the craftsman. Colors applied in different thicknesses on the block, as well as juxtaposition of different colors on one block, lead to fine picturesque effects and the gentlest transitions that cause us to forget the brittleness of the materials.

These colored sheets were not regarded at all as representing a high form of art. They were quite simply products of an artistic craft that could be bought everywhere very cheaply. When, in the middle of the nineteenth century, the Japanese opened the gates of their previously strictly guarded country to Europeans, these colored woodcuts gradually became known throughout the world, after having been known in their countries of origin for more than a thousand years, even if not in their subsequent degree of colorfulness. It was not always the case that one artist carried out all the work from sketch to finished print. Often the painter, the man who cut the block, and the printer were three different persons who worked jointly on the woodcut with a fine degree of artistic sensitivity.

The spreading of these Japanese colored woodcuts was of inestimable importance for the whole of European graphic art. We also find echoes of Japanese models in the "Art Nouveau" which dominated not only graphic art, but also architecture and the applied arts for decades. The development of applied art in particular owes much to these oriental colored prints. The French painter Toulouse-Lautrec, beyond doubt, received very strong inspiration from the Japanese woodcut, and he is rightly regarded as the forerunner of modern poster art. Realism in drawing, the boldness and sureness in the lines, and the perfect sense of design and movement which, apart from cultivated coloring, characterize Japanese woodcuts, provided new impulses to all European painting at the turn of the century. (See also supplement plates VII and VIII)

The art of the Japanese woodcut may be divided into two epochs. These are: the early period, which ended at about the beginning of the nineteenth century; and the later period, which comprises all such works created since then. The main section of the later period lies between about 1830 and 1860. The principal Japanese artists of the time were Hiroshige, Kunisada, Kuniyoshi, and Hokusai. (See also supplement plates X and XI)

Equipment for woodcuts

The block can be made from various materials. The name "woodcut" is, after all, only a collective term for this technique which is used not only in wood and linoleum, but also in metal or plastic materials. The woodblock itself varies according to the nature of the work. Pear, beech, cherry, poplar, and also the soft and supple linden are used. The choice of material cannot usually be seen from the final woodcut print. This is not so, however, if the artist deliberately takes into account the grain of the wood in order to obtain a special effect, as was sometimes done by Emil Nolde (1867–1956) or by the Norwegian Edvard Munch (1863–1944).

If only hand prints are to be made from the block, its thickness does not matter; but if it is intended to be printed on a press, then the block must be a little under an inch thick. This size corresponds in all printing machines to the height of the letters. Linoleum blocks are, for this reason, made up to the correct thickness by sticking them onto a suitable wooden plate.

The cutting tools, such as the gouge, scrive, and knife (for linoleum also a cutting pen) conform to the block which is chosen. Scrives of various widths are intended for working in wood cut across the grain. This is used for particularly fine woodcut work (wood engraving). Definite instructions for the use of narrow and wide gouges are not necessary, since people will choose the tools that suit their intentions. After all, there have been artists who have produced artistic work with the humblest of materials. A pocketknife and a piece of linden or poplar have sufficed on occasion.

Further tools are the **scraper** and **pad.** The first serves for rubbing the printing pigment on a glass or stone plate prior to printing. The pad, which can easily be made from wool or wadding and a piece of thin waste leather, serves for applying the color to the block if one does not wish to use a handy **rubber roller** (gelatine roller) for this.

Wood cut along the grain

Linoleum block

Wood cut across the grain

Scrives

Knife

Gouges

Scraper

Pad

Set-screw

Rubber

Roller for applying pigment

Pressure roller

Burnisher

147

Outline drawing from nature, serving as pattern for a four-color woodcut

The tracing which is applied in reverse onto the wood or linoleum block

The first block for the colored woodcut (black block), which also forms the basis for further colors

150

Yellow block for the four-color woodcut

Red block for the four-color woodcut

Blue block for the four-color woodcut

Composite print of the four-color woodcut

Japanese woodcut

Japanese woodcut showing the extremely fine watercolorlike blendings

Color and Black-and-White Lithography

Although lithography had been known earlier, at the end of the eighteenth century Aloys Senefelder discovered the lithographic transfer process. Since lithography was able only then to acquire its full importance and efficiency, he is rightly considered its pioneer.

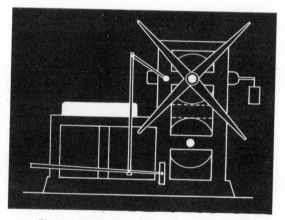

The first lithographic press made by Senefelder

The name "lithography," which means "writing on stone," indicates the most important material used. It is a carbonaceous limestone, the surface of which has to be ground quite even and smooth. Not all limestone can be used, but only that found in Solnhofen, Bavaria. Its hardness and color vary; there are stones of bright yellow, gray-blue, and almost black. Depending on the technique to be used, stones of various degrees of hardness are chosen: for example, for work in pen technique a not too soft yellow stone, and for drawings with chalk or crayon a harder stone.

The oldest and, at the same time, also the most tedious way of drawing on stone is the pen technique. The lithographic stone is ground absolutely flat and smooth, using water, abrasive sand, and pumice, either by a hand pestle or a grinding machine, and is then rinsed clean. After complete drying, the outlines of the drawing are transferred to the stone, using gelatine tracings; and thereafter all details of the drawing are drawn in clearly with lithographic ink, which consists for the most part of fat, soap, and lampblack.

A certain popularity is enjoyed, particularly in color lithography, by the so-called pen-point method with which even chalk tones can be imitated. This method is, however, extremely tiresome for it has to be done point by point with the pen.

A technique far more often used by artists is chalk or crayon drawing. The quite smoothly ground stone must, in this case, be grained before use. The stone-grinder grains with finer or coarser sand by moving another stone over the surface of the first, thus making it rough. The good effect of the drawing depends on this "grain," since on a flat grain drawings become indistinct and lack powerful depth. Lithographic crayon is made from similar constituents to the ink. As a result of its application, a drawing containing fat is formed which is, like the ink, insoluble in water.

For preparing uniformly toned and shaded areas, hardened gelatine sheets are used into which a special pattern (for example, of points or lines in a variety of forms) has been sharply embossed, so that it protrudes in relief on the reverse side, as in a relief printing plate. This patterned film stretched in a frame is rolled with ink, laid with the blackened side on the stone, and transferred to the stone by passing a rubber over it or, in the case of smaller drawings, by rubbing with a burnisher. All parts of the drawing that are not intended to receive the pattern are previously covered with a paper template. The shaded area can still be drawn over as desired with a pen or crayon. After the drawing has been applied to the stone, the latter has to be etched, that is, the surface of the stone has to be made capable of printing by the application of a solution of gum arabic which has been mixed with weak nitric acid. The acid rubber solution is allowed to remain on the surface for a few minutes, as a result of which it penetrates into the pores of the stone. When the solution is rinsed off with water, the still moist surface of the stone is covered with a little turpentine. It will then be found that the drawing is dissolved and finally disappears completely. This is, however, only apparently the case. In reality, the fatty constituents of the crayon have been absorbed into the pores of the stone. The turpentine is now also washed off with water. The stone remains damp and can only now be rolled with lithographic ink. Then the **mirror image** of the picture appears as a clear black drawing. If a sheet of paper is laid on it and pressed down, the final picture or lithograph is formed. The stone should be moistened and rolled before each print is taken off.

The color is sold as "lithograph color." When buying it, care must be taken to ask for chalk or pen color, depending on the drawing technique.

In order to obtain a large number of perfect pictures on a lithographic press, it is necessary to prepare the surface of the stone several times, to etch somewhat more strongly than is necessary for hand printing. Printing is seldom carried out from the original plate, this normally being done only in cases of large drawings and small editions. For machine printing, transfers are usually made, their number being based on the size of the edition. One picture about 20 × 30 cm in size in an edition of ten thousand copies will require at least four transfers, so that the actual number of prints for each would amount to only twenty-five hundred. The larger the edition, the more transfers are made, using the most favorable machine sizes. The transfer is made in the following manner. As many pulls are made as transfers are needed from the etched and inked stone, using transfer color on transfer paper, of which there are suitable sizes for various purposes, and these transfers are pierced so that they fit exactly onto the correctly divided so-called format sheet. This sheet is then laid with the pulls – picture-side down – onto the smoothly ground, moist stone, covered with a pressure board, and the whole is drawn through the press several times with increasing tension. As a result of the high pressure and because the prepared side of the transfer paper contains starch, the pulls remain sticking to the stone and the piercing sheet can easily be drawn off. When finally the transfer paper is softened with warm water and the remains of the starch are completely washed away, the pulls of the drawing stand out clearly and sharply on the stone, which is now etched and inked exactly as described above. If the original is to be reversed, that is, if what appears on the right of the picture is to appear on the left, then a so-called "counter-transfer" is made. The transfer pulls are then again drawn over the transfer paper and only these pulls are transferred onto the stone.

Corrections are easier to carry out in lithography than in any other technique. If something on the transferred drawing has to be omitted, this part is simply scraped away with an appropriate instrument and the corrected place is then etched. If something has to be changed on the transfer or is to be added, then it is first necessary to make the etched stone able to receive color again at this point or to "deacidify" it, as the experts say. This is done by dabbing at the spot in question with citric acid or a solution of alum. The stone now accepts color and ink again at the deacidified spots, and the drawing can be added to with pen and ink or the correct piece of drawing can be printed in by transfer. After the correction has been completed, the stone is etched again.

If it is a question of the reproduction of multicolored work, a different stone is, of course, required for each desired color. In order to obtain an exact matching up of the colors when printing, it is necessary to draw in so-called register crosses on each plate. If these crosses are in exactly the right position on each stone, then matching is assured in the composite print. As in all other reproductive techniques, multicolored effects can be obtained in lithography by overprinting various colors.

A zinc plate may be used in place of stone. Its treatment is the same as for stone in drawing and etching. An aluminium plate can also be processed in the same way.

This method of reproducing drawings has persisted to the present day, and there was a time (around the turn of the century) when lithography celebrated real triumphs. Even if lithography has lost some of its importance for industry, not least as a result of the perfection of offset printing and the manufacture of printing blocks, the commercial artist and illustrator still turn to it today with pleasure.

The transfer paper mentioned above is more convenient than the heavy stone, so that drawing is understandably done on this material. For the same reason today there is also a preference for the metal plate as the support for the drawing, from which direct duplicating is then possible by the offset process. When transfer paper or a metal plate is used for offset work, the artist also has the advantage of being able to draw the correct way round, since both printing processes first transfer the picture in reverse onto the sheet of paper, and then by transfer to the stone or (as in offset printing) by intermediate printing onto rubber, the correct picture again confronts us in the final result. There was a time (around the turn of the century) when transfer drawing in lithography was widely attacked as unoriginal. Lawsuits were even based on this strange view. We cannot understand this attitude today since, in the final analysis, an artistic process is required, without regard to any of the mechanical influences and aids that are used more and more in the interests of progress in reproductive techniques.

Innumerable different ways of drawing on stone have been developed in the course of time. The technique allows blendings in drawing, in addition to a covered area, and a scraping technique reminiscent of wood engravings.

A special place among the various techniques of drawing on stone is taken by **etching on stone,** which is less often practiced today. This does not involve engraving with a needle in polished stone as in stone engraving. Using a covering of asphalt, as in real etching on copper and zinc, etching on stone is carried out with a needle. It is much easier to work freely in the thin layer of asphalt than in stone engraving, and etching also allows softer treatment and greater modulation of the drawing.

Emil Orlik, Portrait of a woman, lithograph

Etching on stone overprinted with a tinted plate

Poster lithographed in two colors

Decorative drawing on stone in two colors

We may also mention here the scraping technique, a type of original lithography that results in very effective prints. The suitably grained stone is, as in etching on stone, provided with a layer of asphalt. The drawing sketch is traced onto this layer, and working is gradually carried out from the dark to the bright sections. The more material we scrape away at one point in the stone, the smoother the stone becomes and the brighter these parts appear in the print. A needle can also be used for working on the stone. When the process of scraping and drawing is finished, the stone is gummed and etched.

Stained Glass

This is the art of making ornamental and painted sheets of glass. Either color-less sheets of glass are painted and fired, or pieces of glass are manufactured in colors according to a preliminary sketch and are worked into a picture, using lead to join them.

Stained glass has been known since the eleventh century. Initially it was, and still is, used for church windows, the technical methods remaining unchanged for several centuries. The colored pieces of glass are put together to form ornaments and figures after the manner of a mosaic. Large Gothic church windows were made in this way in the fourteenth and fifteenth centuries. There were at that time traveling workshops for stained glass, which settled where they found sufficient work for a prolonged period, possibly on the construction of a cathedral. Since the sixteenth century stained glass has also been used for decorating ordinary buildings. Since the time of the Renaissance, however, the feeling for the original character of the art of composite colored fragments has been lost to an ever greater extent.

The beauties and importance of stained glass have once again been recognized in our day. As was the case long ago, the brightly colored fragments serve today for decorating churches and public buildings. The specialization of past centuries is, naturally, no longer sought. In the past there used to be exclusively architectural painters, painters of flowers, flesh and so on, who were assigned to the appropriate section of a church window. This specialization has disap-peared, and where artistic works in stained glass are now carried out, the artist who created the idea will also design the cartoon, choose each piece of colored glass himself, and even fit together the pieces like a transparent mosaic onto a sheet of rough glass, using sticking wax. Then each of the further processes from firing to leading will be supervised by him in the interests of a homogeneous work of art.

Thorn-Prikker, St. Michael (glass window)

166

While in previous centuries the masters of stained glass created their miracles of color with only a few basic colors and shades, today a very large number of different shades is available, thanks to the achievements of color chemistry. This explains why, in contrast to earlier times, the use of mixtures with metal oxides can increasingly be avoided during the melting process.

There is scarcely a material as rich as glass in its diversity and legendary

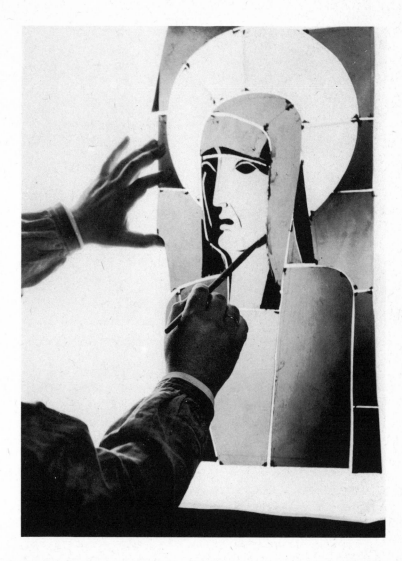

When the sheets of glass are cut, they are stuck with sticking wax onto a clear sheet of glass. The painter can then add the additional sections of the painting with a liquid called black solder

Both the numbered pieces of glass and the thickness of the lead are marked in on the outline tracing. The pieces of glass are first leaded to one another loosely according to these indications

significance. It resembles the surface of a sheet of water in which all things are refracted; it is at the same time a conclusion and a beginning. Light should dominate creations in stained glass and, as a result, confer a special character on the edifice.

When making paintings on glass, as on porcelain, earthenware, or majolica, a permanence and constancy can be obtained that cannot be achieved by other methods of painting. The painting itself will last as long as the material on which it was carried out. There are examples of these arts which are centuries old, having been painted on wellfired pottery, porcelain, and earthenware. In real stained glass the pigments are mixed in the form of a very fine powder with the so-called glass flux or molten glass. Enough oil of turpentine or oil of lavender is then added to the mass for a liquid to be formed which can be spread, this being applied to a glass surface with a brush. One difficulty when painting is the previous calculation of the color effect, since a certain change cannot be avoided when firing the colors. Surprises can only be prevented by carrying out small tests on pieces of glass on which various pigment samples are applied and fired as the real glass sections will be later.

When the individual parts of the window (generally not larger than 1.5 square meters) are put together, leading of the joins is necessary

Many colors and color effects occur only during firing in the kiln at a very high temperature. These kilns, called muffle furnaces, contain chambers or muffles made of fireproof material, such as clay. They serve for heating or firing pigments on glass or porcelain.

The heating of these muffles should take place quite slowly, in order that there may be no cracking of the sheets of glass. Once a certain degree of heat is reached, the fire is increased to a certain extent to allow the "flux" to melt completely. Then the muffle is slowly cooled to a lower temperature, so that the glass can cool slowly without being damaged. The pigments are now completely embedded in the glass plate, for the "flux," which is itself glass, coalesces completely with the glass plate. This also explains the permanence of stained glass.

Section of a glass window showing the formation of bubbles and toning of the colored glass, in other words its structure, as well as the varying thickness of the leading and (on the hand) modern stained glass technique with black solder

Colored design for a glass window

Erhardt Klonk, Section of a cartoon for a window depicting Christ, in the chancel of the "Stiftsberg" in Herford (1955)

Erhardt Klonk, Window in a staircase

Martin Koblo, Design for a colored window

174

13th Century window in the Elizabeth Church in Marburg (property of the Museum)

14th Century stained glass window in Frankfurt/M. Städel Institut

Glass Painting

From late antiquity up to the high Renaissance glass painting was one of the esteemed arts. It was a special type of glass painting for which opaque, that is, nontransparent, oil pigments were used. On one surface of a sheet of glass, the reverse outline of a drawing is carried out in color, and the resultant areas are then painted in. Upon drying the painting is covered with a final layer of varnish. This method is certainly the simplest and most primitive glass painting, such as is practiced today only in isolated instances in remote villages. Sometimes the outlines are first sized and filled in with Dutch gold, and occasionally the background of the glass painting is coated with mercury, so that the picture appears as though it had been painted on a mirror.

Besides the oil pigment technique, the painting can also be undertaken with tempera pigments. In this case it has to be provided with a coating for protection against moisture (oil color, or a coat of varnish, or by pasting over the glass painting).

A further technique of glass painting consists in the use of various layers of color that are applied successively on the back of the plate of glass. This involves underpaintings of the picture, stressing all the details of the drawing and color gradations, and finally there is a surface overpainting of all these details of drawing and color. In contrast to painting on other grounds, glass painting is undertaken in **reverse** order: the highest light first, then the shadow sections and finer gradations of shade, and finally the basic tone. Viewed through the glass, the underpainting of course appears to us as overpainting in the finished work. It is obvious that in this painting in layers a drying of each layer is essential, since otherwise a dissolution of the color would damage the painting. It is recommended that each layer of color be provided with a layer of varnish, before applying a further coat of color.

The preparation of a rustic glass painting in the order of application of the color can be seen from the illustrations on the following pages.

Figure on page 179

The outline drawing, for the execution of which, as an aid, a sketch on the scale 1:1 is fixed onto one side of the sheet of glass with adhesive film. We must be clear beforehand that the finished painting shows a picture "in reverse."

Figure on page 180

The various surfaces indicated show the colors which lie, as it were, as a second layer over the outline drawing.

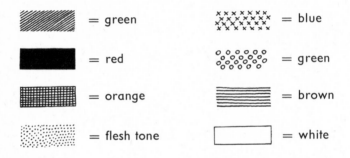

Figure on page 181 (left)

The colors which have been painted as a third layer on the sheet of glass.

Figure on page 181 (right)

The covered bright green area as a final touch to the glass painting.

Figure on page 182

The finished glass painting.

179

These small and modest rustic glass paintings represent mainly religious themes. Without making any claim to be really artistic productions, the sometimes quite colorful representations of Biblical content were not intended to be anything other than modest devotional pictures. The genuine and original naivete expressed in the small painted sheets of glass, when compared with other types of painting, has something of dreams and folksongs about it.

The technique of glass painting has often also been used for votive pictures. These are mostly made by unskilled peasant hands and carried out as the fulfillment of a vow **(ex voto),** or they may report on or warn against accidents, sometimes in a drastic manner. Tradition has it that the Romans spread the votive picture in Europe, but such votive tablets also occur in Buddhist art.

Characteristic of these religious glass paintings is the decided disregard of depth, which is not expressed at all in a large number of these tablets. As in pictures by medieval painters, who did not practice the convincing reproduction of three-dimensional objects on a two-dimensional picture surface, rustic glass painting stresses only the surface.

182

Sgraffito (sgraffiare = to scratch)

This type of wall painting, which has today been revived in Italy, Switzerland, Austria, and also in southern Germany, was popular at the time of the Renaissance. It is a technique in which cutting out or scratching is performed from one or more different superimposed layers of plaster. A dark-colored layer of plaster is applied to the wall which is to be "painted," with a further different colored layer being applied to this while it is still fresh. There may be two or more layers of plaster. Since the plaster is cut out by means of a knife or knife-like scraper, the applied layers have to be worked on in the fresh state, since this would no longer be possible once the layers set. The whole work must, therefore, be carried out in a few days. Either a dark drawing is formed on a bright ground or a bright drawing on a dark ground, depending on the position of the layers of plaster. The preparation of the first ground, the under-plaster, serves not only to smooth the wall, but is at the same time the ground for the scratching. The last layer, the so-called covering layer, must be the same shade as the plaster layer of the façade or room. The individual layers are colored by mineral pigments.

As in every type of wall painting, a true-to-scale sketch is necessary before sgraffito work is begun. The drawing of the selected subject must be simplified, and the lines must show a clear and uncomplicated method of reproduction corresponding to the technique. The coloring of the sketch must also harmonize with the architecture of the room or the façade. The enlarging of the sketch or the drawing of the cartoon then begins, this being done on a 1:1 scale. The enlarging is performed most conveniently by means of the reliable grid system, transferring the drawing from small squares into correspondingly larger ones. This enlarged drawing is then transferred to the wall.

In contrast to fresco painting, which has richer pictorial possibilities of expression, sgraffito technique provides a particularly weatherproof process which is not so easily liable to deteriorate. Care should, however, be taken that the application of the individual colored layers of plaster is entrusted to a skilled workman. As in fresco painting, a test on a sample wall is recommended before carrying out the actual sgraffito work.

Sgraffito ornament of a china vase

The technique of sgraffito extends not only to the ornamentation of walls, but this process was also used by the Chinese more than eight hundred years ago for decorating vases and other vessels. Here the drawing appeared in the brown shade of the clay ground and thus contrasted effectively with the actual bright color of the vessel. The people of Asia, who have always known how to handle a brush, decorated these ceramic products with the same obvious skill in this scratching technique with ornamental lines.

A parallel to the sgraffito technique is found in "rough cast," which has been used for centuries to decorate timber-framed houses. Such decorations are today, of course, often carried out by skilled workers, but the idea behind these ingenious decorations was no doubt derived from the ancient need to ornament with various patterns and shapes.

184

Multicolored sgraffito work on the wall of a house

Rough-cast ornament using traditional shapes

Mural Painting

1. Al fresco painting, or painting on fresh plaster

In this extremely ancient method of painting, the fresh lime contained in the ground plays the part of a binding agent. Only as much new ground may, therefore, be applied to the wall to be painted as the artist can cover with pigment in one day. For this reason, the preliminary drawing cannot be carried out in full size as in other painting techniques. This is a method of painting which can be done in sections only. It entails an adequate amount of preliminary work on a cartoon before beginning the fresco painting, the cartoon serving as the plan for the actual mural. This preliminary drawing is divided up into separate planned daily amounts and is accordingly traced on in sections only. Fresco painting can be considered as the main technique of monumental painting. Working with water-soluble powdered pigments, which soon bind insolubly with the layer of lime mixed with quartz sand, requires a rapid and bold execution. For this reason exaggerated details have to be dispensed with in the interests of a painting which has, by its nature, been oriented to distant viewing. The fact that the pigments become lighter on drying must also be taken into account when planning the work. In order for the colors to appear in their intended force and effectiveness in the finished painting, the artist must determine exactly how much each color will lose in intensity after drying. This is possible only after a series of practical tests.

The outline is particularly important in mural painting. It is, after all, a type of painting which is primarily dependent on the contour. This does not alter at all the splendid colors of the individual areas, as is, for example, clearly shown in the famous frescoes by Giotto in the Arena Chapel in Padua. The composition

Giotto (1266–1337). This extremely gifted and important Italian painter is considered a great revolutionary in western art. The element that was quite novel in his time was the emotional depth of expression, which deviates from customary Byzantine formalism and leads towards the Renaissance. His

method of composition, the three-dimensional design of the picture, and the magnitude and dignity of his representations of people make Giotto a pioneer of all European painting. Our illustrations show sections from his frescos "From the Life of Mary and Christ" (Arena Chapel, Padua)

also has to be matched in form and color to the architectural conditions. Mural painting should be the servant of architecture and, in this way, itself become part of a building.

The ground is a mixture of lime paste (slaked lime) and sand. The lime paste has a certain adhesive power, even when stirred with sand (mortar), so that the plaster can be spread with a mason's trowel and adheres to the wall. Through the action of air, this mortar plaster loses its excess water and the drying process begins. When the mortar hardens, the water separated out from the hydrate of lime gradually evaporates on the surface. It is not, however, pure water; because of the solubility of the hydrate of lime, it becomes lime water, which deposits its lime content on the surface, where a crystal film of calcium carbonate (calcareous sinter) is formed. At the same time the pigment layer on the mortar ground is pervaded by this lime water, so that the painting also acquires a crystal coating of calcium carbonate. This is the reason why fresco pigments dry brightly.

After the day's work, the unpainted remainder of plaster has to be removed again. After this, a section of the painting is chosen onto which the new layer of plaster can be applied without difficulty on the next day. The permanence of fresco painting depends largely on the nature of the mortar ground. One condition is a dry wall surface that cannot absorb any moisture from the soil. Before undertaking such a painting, we must be sure that this fault will not occur. Imperfect bricks that may even contain salpeter will destroy the plaster as well as the whole painting because of crystalline excretions (wall corrosion).

The lime for mixing the plaster must be well seasoned. Under no circumstances should freshly slaked lime be used.

The sand for the mortar should be pure quartz or marble sand, without any clay content (washed sand).

An extremely ancient and proven method is to apply several layers of mortar. Each layer must, however, be well dried before the next is applied. The last coat, the actual painting layer, should be about four to five millimeters thick. Since the application of the plaster is, in general, a matter for the mason, it is recommended that, before beginning a mural painting, all these requirements should be made clear. Cement mortar is not suitable for fresco paintings, since this mixture of plaster does not include the fixing of the pigments. An addition of gypsum to the mortar should also be avoided.

Picture of Christ in the cupola of a Byzantine church in Greece

Only those pigments should be chosen which are resistant to light. Lead and copper pigments are to be avoided if possible, since they are sensitive to hydrogen sulfide. Yellow chromium pigments, lakes, and Prussian blue (Paris blue) are thoroughly harmful, because they are destroyed by the action of lime. A solution of marble dust and milk of lime may, for example, be used as a white.

Frost is one of the main enemies of fresco painting. No work of this type can in the long run withstand the effects of cold, and many a masterpiece has been ruined by the influence of cold weather.

2. Al secco (mural painting with water-soluble pigments on a dry wall plaster)

This is the technique of mural painting that is mainly used today. It is a type of tempera painting carried out on dry plaster, in contrast to al fresco technique. The al secco process is also used for retouching al fresco paintings, particularly when subsequently conferring greater depth on certain shadow sections and dark colors. A glazing can scarcely be considered here, since dirty and foreign sections would certainly result within the fresco painting. In the case of such corrections a dotting or pointing will be chosen that can be worked in with the original ground. There should be no attempt to alter or improve the lights of a fresco painting with tempera pigment. The luminosity of the colors, which have an almost watercolor character, would only lose in beauty through any such tempera retouching.

3. Casein tempera painting

Casein is a protein obtained from the milk of mammals. This casein which is contained in milk separates out with the addition of acid (acetic acid). A milk that is poor in fat (skim milk) is used for this, and the casein is obtained as a thick mass, quite similar to milk that has turned sour of its own accord by the transformation of milk sugar or lactose into lactic acid. For preparing casein from skim milk, rennet obtainable from druggists may also be used. (Ferment from rennet = two tea spoons to about one pound skim milk.) This mixture is heated to about 102° and the thick mass of casein is obtained in about two minutes. The aqueous constituents which contain protein are removed by pressing it through a cloth.

192

12th Century fresco painting (St. Panteleymon Church, Nerezine)

The casein (white cheese) obtained in this way can now be transformed by various solvents into a sticky liquid, so that a binding agent for pigments is formed. Casein can be hardened and ground by using a suitable drying process, powdered casein being formed in this way.

The use of pigments bound with casein has since the earliest times been directed principally to mural painting, and painting with casein pigments has continued to be used up to the present day. Apart from the wall as a ground, this technique is also used in panel painting. For this purpose the casein tempera is given a certain degree of suppleness by the addition of drying oils that help to reduce the tension when the pigments dry. Linseed oil, varnish, and poppy oil are useful for this. When linseed oil and casein tempera are combined, there is great danger of yellowing.

The prepared casein tempera products available today have proved better for painting rooms than for exterior work. Here, as in all mural painting techniques, the conditions of the ground are important to the success of the painting, and tests in this technique will first have to be carried out before undertaking such work.

Reference should also be made to the fact that non water-soluble casein tempera pigment is suitable as an underpainting pigment for oil painting as well as for egg tempera paintings.

A wall picture must differ from a panel painting through the composition and the economy of means. Simplifications in the treatment of color and drawing can evince a thoroughly graphic character. The contour or linear element can result in a monumental effect, when combined with carefully graded areas of color.

The artistic execution of a mural painting, therefore, always requires a bold simplified conception directed to an effect of distance. In this way, the painting can, as during the Baroque period, suggest imaginary dimensions to the observer. All possibilities of perspective were explored in the compositions of Baroque painting, and every means was used to extend the depth.

This art of simulating space is, however, opposed by a decidedly two-dimensional type of painting without any illusion of space, for example, in the works of Hodler and Matisse. This same juxtaposition of figures in which modeling is merely suggested can also be seen in older paintings and mosaics. The renunciation of depth gives these wall paintings a certain immediacy and directness. As regards depth, however, Giotto was the first to influence Italian painting through his plastic shaping of a picture.

Roman wall paintings from the first century B. C. are known which, apart from a skillful modeling of light and shadow, already show foreshorteings that create the idea of space. They contrast with Etruscan creations and Egyptian wall paintings, which stress merely a two-dimensional range.

Tiepolo, Section of a ceiling fresco in the staircase of the Würzburg Residence (1752–1753)

Sketch based on a fresco study by Fritz Erler. The uneven nature of the wall has been taken into account in this preliminary study

Giotto (1266–1337), whose frescoes today still arouse universal admiration, overcame the Byzantine tradition. A hundred years later Masaccio (1401–1428) used Giotto's style, but he endeavored to obtain a realistic reproduction of figures. In the Middle Ages and Renaissance it was the Italian painters who acquired a world reputation with their mural paintings. Ghirlandaio (1449–1494), Signorelli (1441–1523), Raphael (1483–1520), and later Michelangelo

Ferdinand Hodler, Sketch based on a plan for "Eurhythmy"

(1475–1564) were the chief painters whose frescoes have remained, down to the present, an attraction for many visitors interested in art. Their views and knowledge formed an example, a stimulus, and a standard.

Among the creations of more recent date, there are two painters in particular whose monumental style has exerted a decisive and determining influence. In the south it was the Swiss Ferdinand Hodler (1853–1918) and in the north the Norwegian Edvard Munch (1863–1944) who had a very marked effect on European painting. The representational world of both painters was derived from the problems of life. The expressive force of their works flowed from their use of area, symmetry, linear rhythm, with strong simplification in the case of Hodler, and with depth of expression, demonic elements, and a colorful intoxicating rendition of experience in the case of Munch. Both painters, together with Van Gogh and Cézanne, can be regarded as among the fathers of modern painting. (See also supplement plates XII and XIII)

Ferdinand Hodler, Sketches for "The Disappointed Ones"

A mural painting should not be satisfied with showing only sections, as is possible with panel painting. The action should affect the observer clearly and plainly through the composition. The architecture of a space must remain the main consideration. A finely arranged architectural scheme requires a corresponding treatment of color and form; heavy architecture is best coupled with monumentality and the simplest stylization. The fact that rooms of small dimensions can also be well decorated with mural paintings is evident from many graceful ornamental and figure representations from ancient Pompeii. In our day, on the other hand, it is abstract art which has almost unlimited opportunities for development in the field of mural painting, insofar as it is a question of decorative creation.

Mosaic

Mosaic technique can be regarded as painting with stones. It is actually an indirect type of painting, apart from the fact that the preliminary work for it comes directly within the field of painting. Presentday architecture employs more and more decorative mosaics in ornamental or figurative form. With the sobriety of our new buildings these colored and decorative surface treatments are a welcome interruption to unrelieved façades and walls. From a technical point of view, nothing has changed in this technique since the Early Christian period.

Ravenna with its mosaic treasures represents to the world the quintessence of mosaic art. Special riches of early Christian and Byzantine mosaic work, whose unbroken luminosity still continues to shine in its original splendor, are kept in museums. It seemed for a long time as if mosaic would die out until, at the end of the last century, this very ancient technique began to be practiced again. A method of painting was sought which would fully withstand all influences of weathering and which would be insensitive to dampness and variations in temperature, and the result was the rediscovery of mosaic.

The dolphin mosaic (floor mosaic) from Delos, Greece

The technical principle behind such permanent mural decorations is centuries old, while the material and its method of use take many forms. Various types of stone, clay, and glass were and still are the most common materials of the artist in mosaic. Apart from the glazed clay plate facings in Assur and Babylon, we have wall and floor mosaics preserved from the Roman period in Pompeii, Rome, and on Germanic soil. Mosaic has enjoyed its greatest blossoming since the fourth century A. D., when it was used for the designing of Christian churches. The large series of figures, the lively stories of the mosaics of Rome and Ravenna have fulfilled the formal laws of this art without parallel up to the present day. Only with real ability and long practice can one discover the correct blend between the surface-bound starkness of a clear drawing in the smooth material and the colored surface which is broken up into a thousand individual parts and which we are seeking again today. The technical possibilities at present are rather wider than in the past. Glass mosaic is the commonest form; its materials are obtained from approximately one centimeter thick "glass cakes" that are uniformly penetrated with pigment. A special group consists of gold or silver mosaic, in which gold or silver leaf lies below fine molten covering glass. Clay stick mosaic, mosaic glazing, and marble mosaic for external surfaces are rarer.

Ravenna with its mosaic treasures is to the world the quintessence of mosaic art. Special riches of Early Christian and Byzantine mosaics, whose undimmed luminosity still continues to shine, are preserved in museums. Our picture shows a section from a ceiling mosaic in Ravenna

An experienced workman with a pick breaks small pieces from the colored glass, which is about the size of a plate. More than fifteen hundred shades are available to the artist as working material. The small stones are fitted side by side to form pictures with figures; the process first takes place in reverse on a cartoon sketch. This sketch is covered with paste, and the picture is assembled on that coating. After drying, the picture in reverse is then pressed into moist cement, so that the cartoon only needs to be softened and removed, and the stones must be cleaned of paste. We then have the finished correct mosaic picture before us.

The same effects transmitted to us by brightly colored stones under the name "mosaic" are quite possible with other materials. Today plastic products are used alongside the original stones. As in other techniques, the final effect determines the relevance of the technique in each case, irrespective of the materials used. The mosaic design should already evoke the technique. A flat bristle brush is very suitable for this work. The rectangular areas can be dabbed on exactly with it, these later forming the real mosaic in the shape of glass stones or other material.

An absolutely finished impression can be obtained in our draft of the mosaic by using pieces of colored paper or cardboard. For this purpose suitable pieces are covered with color, and after drying these are cut into fragments about one square centimeter in size. When these little "stones" are stuck on, it is possible to achieve an effect that largely corresponds to the final work, apart from the gloss of the real stones. Care should be taken, when laying the colored rectangles, that they are not placed strictly vertically and horizontally. It is the change in the rhythm of the stones which produces such charming effects of color and movement. For example, the areas of a figure may be treated differently, when laying the stones, from the way this may possibly be done in the background. In making a wall mosaic, the individual stones can also be set at different levels or depths in the ground. Again, it is possible for the outline to stand out more than the surface treatment of the figures or decoration. Particularly stressed areas can also be made to project in this way.

The nature of the mosaic ground may be as different as the material used for mosaic stones. The deciding factor is, in the final analysis, the purpose and size of the work. A cement ground is used in most cases. The ratio of cement to sand is 1:1, and the mixture stirred with water to give a tough mass. For smaller mosaic works the stucco technique has proved very useful. For this a glass plate is used, under which a tracing in reverse of the design can be laid. With the "picture side" downwards, the stones are now stuck onto the glass plate with a **water-soluble** adhesive, each stone being separated from the next by a space of about two millimeters. Once all the mosaic stones have been placed

Byzantine Madonna (mosaic on wood)

in this way in their predetermined places, the mosaic is enclosed in a temporary wooden frame. Gradually all the spaces are now filled in with fairly thinly stirred plaster of Paris; several applications are sometimes needed. Only after the plaster of Paris has set — and this can take several hours — are the wooden frame and glass plate removed from the actual mosaic picture. The cleaning of the picture should not be begun before it has completely dried. When remains of paste and possible fragments of plaster of Paris have been removed with water and a soft rag, the mosaic can be given a light coating of wax and then polished.

Floor mosaic from Delos, Greece

Mycenaean vase (15th century B. C.)

Decorative Painting

It is apparent from the term itself that this type of painting has in principle an ornamental character. (In contrast to it, we have absolute painting which seeks to make a special statement.) This means that any point or stroke can itself be an ornament or decoration. Decorative painting is not bound to a limitation of subject. Ornaments and figures alternate in bright succession with landscape, just as both nearness to nature and abstraction give it their imprint. It can be said that the possibilities of decorative pictorial design are almost unlimited. Wood and stone, textiles and plastics of all types, metal and glass, all these materials have been provided with ornamental features since the beginning of all culture. Even the human body is no exception, if we think of the painting of the body in very ancient times and of tattooing which is still practiced by many peoples.

If we begin with the simplest geometrical shapes, we already have every possibility of a decorative play of lines or shapes. The triangle, circle, cylinder, rhombus, and so on, have from the start formed the elements of decorative creation. Thus we speak, for example, of a geometrical style of Grecian vases. On the other hand, the shape of animals has provided many models for decorative paintings, to which there may be added the world of plants and of man himself as further subjects. Finally, there are the numerous figures of fable and fantasy to extend the already very wide field. The silhouette plays an important part in all this, occurring as bright on a dark ground and as dark on a bright ground, or also in a continuous alternation of bright and dark. There are symmetrical and asymmetrical arrangements in concepts that are near to nature or abstract. Outlining can be just as much emphasized as it can be dispensed with in favor of pure area. Contrasted as these formulations may be, they nevertheless characterize the essential feature of all decorative art, whose origins are other than life situations.

Apart from these elementary facts, every decorative painting strives for simplification. It is first and foremost the servant of its surroundings, to which it is intended to give a colored accent. A plastic quality in decorative painting is quite unnecessary for its purposes. If this quality should be desired, the distribution of light and shadow may take place without visible transitions. They can be created by adding white and black to the colors in immediate steps, without blending them into one another. Decorative painting, particularly if it is a question of adorning a room or of painting a building, is required to be at a certain distance from the observer. This distance allows the light and shadow sections to appear softer. In this way the eye takes in a plastic form while it supplies for itself the missing element, the gradual transition from light to shadow. The position is the same with the decorative painting of furniture and similar articles. This fact has been made use of principally in the art of posters. Starting from decorative painting, the commercial artist limits himself in his drafting activity to the most essential contrasts only. Such a thor-

Byzantine icon painting. Icon = Greek "image," being in Byzantine art the designation of the movable picture itself. These occurred in Greek art as stylized pictures of the saints on a gold ground

Forms from a painting by Paul Klee

ough simplification, which renounces all unnecessary ballast of form embellishment and color gradation, can lead to a monumental effect.

Panel painting also increasingly includes decorative moments, either in that certain parts of a painting are characterized by them, or in that a greater distance from the picture must be taken into account from the start. Contemporary painting tends towards a conscious turning away from detail. People do not want to be lost in pedantic works, and the resultant broader and more two-dimensionally applied sections of a painting need a greater viewing distance to achieve the unified effect of the picture. The time seems to have passed once and for all when people bent over a charmingly decorated painting with a magnifying glass in order to be able to perceive and study a master's brushstroke. The decorative style of Gauguin and Munch finds an echo in the paintings of the Frenchman Matisse and Marquet. (See also supplement plates XIV and XV). It also expresses itself openly in the paintings of the German **Brücke** group and in the creations of the painters of the **Blauer Reiter** group, who both worshipped an expressively decorative style. This was later to lead to even further simplifications and a more two-dimensionally stressed method of painting, as with Paul Klee (1879–1940) and other painters of this period.

208

Decorative design plays an important part in Chinese painting. Everything is perfection in this art. Movement, balanced areas, and technical ability led to the creation of decorative masterpieces

Decorative design in three colors for a wrapper in which any plastic emphasis has been renounced

Henri Matisse (1864–1954), Portrait (1907). The works of this French painter are characterized by a preference for decorative emphasis

211

Decorative painting (tempera on cardboard)

Christian Rohlfs (1849–1938), Still life with Roses, decorative painting on cardboard

Albert Marquet (1875–1947). The tendency towards the decorative element cannot be denied in Marquet's paintings. In spite of the compact forms they are anything but monotonous. The painting creates its impression through harmony and balance; it is clear, light, and rich in shading

214

Color and Printing

The preperequisite for good printing, apart from perfectly drawn letters, is its legibility. This does not mean that printing becomes clear by the use of large letters. Legibility is increased by a suitable color contrast, the effectiveness of the colors at a distance also playing a considerable part. Experience has shown that black print on a yellow ground is the best color combination for reading. Another effective color combination is red and black. It is recommended, however, that the red contain a considerable proportion of yellow. A brickred combined with black letters likewise gives a harmonious and easily legible color effect. Deep black letters on a dazzling white ground can cause overstraining of the eyes; this is because of the too marked bright-dark contrast. On the other hand, a dark gray on a light yellowish ground is more legible. The following pages show examples of colors that may serve as a standard for determining degrees of legibility. It is, to a certain extent, a graded list based on numerous practical tests.

It is clear from the examples that, in spite of their color contrast, colors of equal value cannot give contrasts in tone and, consequently, legibility is jeopardized. Furthermore, the size of the color areas also influences the combination of colors. Large black areas on a white ground are ugly and result in poor legibility.

Good color effect and, consequently, optical clarity are prejudiced from the start by using several mutually foreign colors. There can easily be too much of a good thing in this direction.

For this reason, the following six principles, which have often been confirmed in practice, should be used. Reference should also be made to the color harmony table on page 67.

msm

1. A powerful gray tone on a white ground can be more pleasant and better to read than a deep black. This, in turn, is found to be more harmonious and legible if the ground is slightly yellowish in tone.

2. A good optical effect depends on the spatial relationship of the amount of print to the area of background. A little print on a larger area always results in better design than vice versa.

3. The use of positive or negative (such as white on black) letters also exerts an influence on the effect of a printing design. Negative print is more difficult to read than positive. If print is to be easily legible, care should be taken, when there is a large amount of text, to have an appropriately wide space between the lines.

4. Particularly large and fat print on a small area is only tolerable to read if there is not too marked a contrast in tone between the print and the colored ground. Fat lines of print, moreover, must be spaced out slightly, that is, there must be a certain distance between the individual letters. Several fat lines of print without sufficient distance between the lines disturb legibility and the general impression.

5. The smaller print is, the clearer it must be in form. A fine delicate print, however, can be very effective when dark on a bright ground, if the arrangement of the print provides for large distances between letters.

6. More than two different styles of print make the design ugly. A good choice of colors cannot alter this fact appreciably. Good harmony and legibility are obtained in designs with a large amount of text by alternating thin and fat lines, if this is permitted by the sense of the writing.

216

ABCDEFGHIJKLMNO
ABCDEFGHIJKLMNO

Black letters on a white ground. Legibility is rendered difficult by the small distance between the lines, although this does help towards creating a good block effect

SENATOR

White print on a black ground. Legibility is rendered easier by a large space between the lines

ABCDEFGHIJKLMNO
ABCDEFGHIJKLMNO
ABCDEFGHIJKLMNO
ABCDEFGHIJKLMNO

Lines of different colors introduce a decorative element into the appearance of print

1 ABCDEFGHIJKLMNO

2 ABCDEFGHIJKLMNO

3 ABCDEFGHIJKLMNO

4 ABCDEFGHIJKLMNO

5 ABCDEFGHIJKLMNO

6 ABCDEFGHIJKLMNO

ABCDEFGHIJKLMNO

7

ABCDEFGHIJKLMNO

8

ABCDEFGHIJKLMNO

9

ABCDEFGHIJKLMNO

10

ABCDEFGHIJKLMNO

11

ABCDEFGHIJKLMNO

12

ABCDEFGHIJKLMNO

13

Modern Painting

The expression "modern" can lead to false conclusions, for a modern painting logically must be opposed to a nonmodern painting. It is, therefore, more correct to speak of a contemporary painting. "Modern" and "nonmodern" are not estimations of value. They are, in reality, only different terms for present and past. New, but not modern, are perhaps certain views concerning execution. Artistic knowledge can be new if it leads to a different choice of color from that previously used. Finally, a chemical pigment can be new, as can some piece of equipment. All this has nothing whatever to do with the concept of art. If it were a question of estimations of value in the formulations "modern" and "non-modern," we would have to reject as bad and old-fashioned everything that was not up-to-date, or was nonmodern. We could sooner say that for the person of our century another way of seeing has been adopted, that today he approves a different conception of color. This change took place slowly, if we disregard the fact that there have at all times been painters who were seeking new paths. We know generations who were anxious to conceal the characteristics of their equipment, namely, the brush. Brush technique was not allowed to show itself. Everything had to appear as if it had been done in one piece. Today we consider it almost necessary, when viewing a painting, to be able to experience its creative details. The brush-stroke tells us about the technical process; it also allows us to observe the temperament of the artist. Yet it is neither technique nor temperament which gives contemporary painting its stamp. The manner of thinking of people in this century has a far greater influence; this alone determines the great separating line between what we call representational art and abstract creation. Pigments and material have basically remained the same as they were centuries ago, and the human eye sees and perceives as it did in the days of a Dürer, Rembrandt, Courbet, or Van Gogh making the widest choice

Ferdinand Hodler, Study for "Day"

of names. All attempts at painting were initially intended to approach nature as closely as possible. This means that the painter tried to reproduce nature, as revealed to him, in such a way that the observer of his picture should feel in the same way as he or should at least understand his view. A revolution in this artistic attitude took place with the discovery of photography when it was realized that there could be no parallels between painting and photography, that the field for both was and is basically different. Perhaps it was precisely through the rise of photography that painting become aware of the necessity of turning away from what we call objective seeing.

A new method of thinking had questioned the place of the old view. Both disastrous World Wars had a share in this, just as have advances in technical matters and, with them, in civilization. It merely appears as if a continually increasing uniformity in artistic creation has become evident at the same time as these technical advances.

It cannot be the purpose of this book to attempt to judge these matters. We will, therefore, try to follow the path that painting has taken throughout the world and that leads to the abstract cult of our days.

Abstract painting

The word "abstract" has today become a catchword. At the same time, it acquires an interpretation which is basically false. This is the opinion that everything which is not a recognizable object comes within the term "abstract." The Latin word "abstrahere" means "to draw away." To undertake an abstraction, therefore, means to leave out many subsidiary circumstances in favor of individual features. It follows from this interpretation that just these individual features would have to lead to a conscious heightening of expression. If now we mean, in painting by abstraction, the deliberate suppression of the representational in favor of a devised image which is composed of line, area, and color, then the result is in opposition to this interpretation. We would thereby have to translate the term "draw away" by "decompose" or "resolve," and it is here that disagreement begins.

In recent years, the works of abstract artists have been represented more than ever before in exhibitions. It can be stated, that abstraction in art is in no way an expression of the last few years. Abstract works, those which have nothing to do with nearness to nature or representation thereof, have existed for about the last fifty years. Among these we include, for example, the works of the Frenchmen Léger and Braque, the works done in the' twenties by the Spaniard Picasso, as well as those by Kandinsky. The circumstance that most of these

222

Pablo Picasso, Woman's head, decorative painting

artists used Cubism as a beginning form of expression does not alter the fact that what took place here was a complete turning away from the representational which led to abstraction.

The signs of an abstract art, be it in a much milder form, can already be recognized in previous centuries. If we follow the history of art, it can be shown that there were in each epoch artists who tried to detach themselves from the art of their time, and whose different findings and observations led to the paving of new paths. Let us just think of Rembrandt who, with advancing age, created more and more powerful works of increasing expressive force, and who thereby withdrew from the works of his contemporaries and those of his own younger years. The public understood and appreciated the late works of Rembrandt less and less, and eventually rejected them completely. We do not wish to recall the many examples from even earlier times which are still extant, but will be content to mention the name of Grünewald, to whom force of expression often meant more than a skilled, anatomically correct representation. Frans Hals surprised his time by his extraordinarily lively and free brushstroke which suggests a premature Impressionism.

Then comes the eighteenth century, the Rococo period, with its playful, somewhat sweet representations, corresponding to the nature of social life at that time. The Englishman Turner may be regarded as an exception here. His paintings, suffused with light, are anything but true representations of nature. Not a little boldness was required for declaring oneself in favor of Turner's manner of viewing objects and using the brush. Here too we can speak of a forerunner of Impressionism. For his time Turner was, in any case, a personality who distinctly removed himself from what was customary. (See also supplement plate XVI)

A hundred years later painting in the open air was heralded as the only true faith. Expressionism followed, superseding Impressionism and setting the subjective method of expression against objective viewing. In contrast to past centuries, one "ism" now suddenly pursued the other, and the question, "What is really the right and valid path for visual art?" was raised more sharply than at any previous time. The answer was, briefly: many paths lead to art, which are all correct and valid, if prerequisites for a work of art are present. By this reasoning, every epoch produces good and bad works, irrespective of whether they are naturalistic, impressionistic, expressionistic, or, in the wider sense, abstract pictures or sculpture. How can one be right if the other is also right? That is the question which is asked when we observe the juxtaposition or succession of individual works with their very different methods of representation.

A work of art, and that seems to me to be the correct standard, is not good because it is naturalistic and not bad because it is abstract. The differences

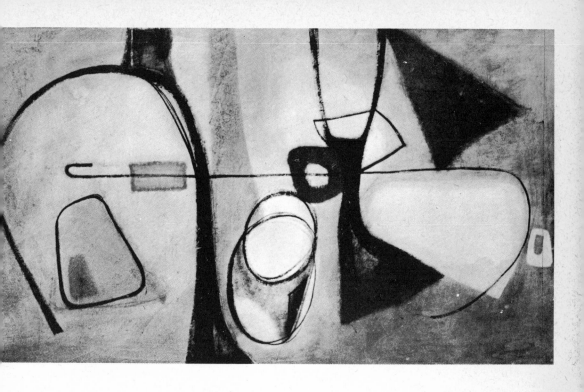

Camaro, Abstract painting

do not, in fact, lie here. Is it easier to judge the quality of a naturalistic or impressionistic picture, pertaining to what is representational, than that of an abstract, nonrepresentational painting? This is, in my opinion, the main point, if not, in fact, the nucleus of the pros and cons. I do not, however, consider a poor naturalistic picture better than any abstract one, merely "because one can at least see what it represents and because one knows how to hang it up." Can we, on the other hand, require an unconditional "yes" from the public who, in most cases, understandably cannot follow directly the artist's line of thought and who, in any case, cannot possess the same knowledge of the matter as the practicing creative artist? I do not think so, and the artist who judges objectively will certainly be of the same opinion. It would be wrong, therefore, to describe a rejection of abstract art, as unfortunately sometimes happens, as philistine and ignorant. Abstractions are also rejected by artists whom we must take quite seriously. To call these people old-fashioned and antiquated, which likewise happens, is unjustified. Current interest is, after all, of no importance for the estimation of a work of art. By this judgment we commit the same error as the visitor to an exhibition who feels the lack of nearness to nature in every case as a lack of art. It follows, then, that representational and nonrepresentational art both have their full justification. There is only a juxtaposition and not merely one true method of expression.

The future will show what will remain of our present-day abstract art and what part of it will pass into the history of art as generally admissible. I said at the beginning of this chapter that abstractions in their present form had been set forth over fifty years ago. This type of art has not been able to develop further in this period. It is a matter of variations on a theme which has so far remained the same.

To many people the position is different if this painting becomes a means to an end, if without any individual expression the compositions of lines, areas, and colors become part of a building, if they remain an ornamental accessory and help to fulfill decorative functions, possibly in a room. In other words, abstractions are admissible as long as they remain part of applied art or architecture, as long as they do not seek to be anything more than an interpolation. They may be beautiful in color and movement and harmonious in composition. We experience the distribution of weight in this case with mathematical exactitude as it was solved. Whether these creations are, however, in a position to arouse the same or similar feelings as, possibly, a portrait by Van Gogh or a landscape by Munch, must be left to the viewer's judgment and estimation.

Abstract forms have in recent years conquered a wide field in commercial art. The same also applies to a considerable number of industrial firms who have, to a large extent, claimed the abstract world of forms for themselves. It may be

226

Léger, Composition

said that today whole branches of industry are profiting indirectly from the strange and magical creations of Paul Klee (1879–1940). Lamp-shades, curtains, carpets, ceramics, porcelain, and so forth, are all products that bear abstract forms as ornamental decoration.

The adherents of abstract painting see in it an absolute in art. This group, therefore, rejects the idea of subordinating this world of forms to be a servant of industrial products. This absolute painting is compared with contemporary creations in music. This is one answer in the search for the organic element in abstract art.

What is Trash?

By the expression, "That is trash!" we assume a rejecting attitude and, consequently, deliver a criticism that indicates contempt.

We who are living today regard as an era of trash particularly the period at the turn of the century. The homes of our grandparents and parents were swamped with an excess of strange objects of daily use. It is not possible to consider all the curiosities that were to be seen. Just think of the artificial flower arrangements that decorated the table in the "best room" (sitting-room) throughout the year, or of the numerous artificial palms. Think also of the pieces of furniture ornamented with stilted shapes and figures, of the flood of "knick-knacks" which covered chests of drawers and cupboards. It was a rich array of make-believe. With these worthless and often pathetic things people wanted to create an impression, and for this they made use of just such futilities. In addition, there were the ubiquitous "crazy" covers and curtains, the mawkish pictures showing romantically dramatic scenes and innumerable other impossible items. We cannot understand today how our forefathers could have felt at ease in this strangely conceived world. And rightly so! All things that appear to be more than they are, give cause for doubt from the start.

We will reject the ash-tray with which is incorporated (perhaps even plastically) the reproduction of, for example, a war memorial or a statue to freedom. The grotesque combination of a small useful object with a national monument (whether it be good or bad from the point of view of construction) is what degrades the object to the level of trash.

Imitations are always to be viewed with caution!

Why, for example, should one want to make gold from wood (that noble material)? And why do this by a banal coating of bronze!

We can, therefore, resignedly use the word "trash" if, for the sake of appearance, a material is modified by falsification with the idea of increasing its value. All overornate decorations, likewise with the intention of helping simple and unpretentious useful objects to assume a more worthy valuable appearance, deserve to be called trash.

Views concerning taste have changed in the meantime, yet no period will be completely free of trivial and trashy creations.

Present-day applied art is endeavoring to create beautiful appropriate forms and is achieving much in this direction. Contemporary architects and furniture-makers are working with realistic and harmonious surfaces and lines, and other industries have in the same way raised their products to a good standard as regards design.

What do we, however, call trash in the visual arts? Here the question is not quite as simple as with everyday objects.

Goethe said "If you do not feel it, then you will not conquer it!" And here too, there applies the saying that one must not place appearance above existence. The painter, for example, who wishes to convince us that he sees all the leaves of a tree in detail, and tries to demonstrate this to us in his drawing, will scarcely be able to convince us of great skill. Every child knows that a tree has many thousands of leaves. A falsely observed and therefore interpreted naturlism does not deserve the description "valuable." The creative person should put his "creative power" to the test by shaping independently, processing and portraying what he sees independently. If there is something in this person, then the result of his work will appeal to us. He will reject tracking down any playful elements. Such a painter or sculptor is not capable of creating trash. A carefully executed drawing or sculpture cannot perhaps be called trash because an artist has cooperated very closely with nature. It can, however, become boring, if the designer has put nothing or only a little of his own contribution into his work. There are situations and things which cannot be brought into direct harmony with the creative hand of man. This is particularly evident in an attempt to create an all too marked "approach to nature." We must free ourselves of the idea that everything can be recreated by us in the "truest way" in a work of art.

The experience of a sunset that we enjoy on top of a mountain can certainly be overpowering. How beautiful it is when the rays of the departing star push through diffused clouds and magically surround the top of the mountain and everything on the earth with the glow of heavenly gold. Yet those who wish to represent these phenomena and reflexes of another world pictorially, as they are seen by the overwhelmed human eye, must fail. Words may be in a position to give a convincing picture of such an experience, without running the danger of becoming ridiculous. The painter who tries to record a sphere which can least of all be captured by naturalistic representation will certainly exceed the limit of what is reasonable according to taste. There are, unfortunately, many examples of this.

It is strange that precisely those who lack the knowledge for recognizing trash give that name to what lies outside the limits of their world of imagination and for which they lack the feeling. There is, therefore, the tendency to deny one's own inability to recognize an artistic work and to denounce as trash what is not understood or felt. This is quite the wrong place for an expression whose characteristic features, namely superficiality and a stereotyped method of representation, merge into irresponsible and very cheap feeling. The fact remains that the all-too-pleasing and all-too-heroic possibly themselves carry the stamp of artistic inadequacy. The purpose of the true artist should also be to have an elevating effect with his work, in that the solidity of his creations leads the public to a higher and more demanding standard.

If we look back into past centuries, it will indeed be difficult for us to find among the artistic works of these eras, which were not encumbered by technology and unrest, such a measure of futilities, which we call by the name trash. It appears that these epochs, which lacked the conveniences of our day, still enjoyed the peace and leisure essential for the creation of a work of art and which the viewer and sympathizer also need to recognize a real and genuine work.

Color Throughout the Centuries

The Stone Age

Stone Age painting was done directly on limestone rocks (for example, the Altamira cave). Various minerals were used as pigments, such as ocher, red iron, manganese black, and lime. Chemical investigations of old colored dishes have shown animal fats, milk, and blood as binding media. The luminosity of the pigments has, in some cases, remained unchanged for thousands of years, but these are indoor paintings that are not resistant to direct moisture and rubbing. Stone Age man obviously knew about the binding and adhesive power of the natural products he used.

Other rock pictures (for example, in North Africa) show paintings that were cut or carved deep into the rock and were then decorated with pigments. These early works, in which the colors ocher, red, white, and black were used, portray mainly animal and hunting scenes. The carved and painted earthenware vessels made in the later Stone Age show paintings which had been carried out with white pigment (lime) plus milk, on fired utensils.

Among the oldest examples of art is the painting of the human body. There are examples of such ornamental decorations on figures engraved on mammoths' teeth which take us back 25,000 years into the past. These paintings by Ice Age men reveal an extraordinary knowledge of the function of the muscles and limbs of the body.

Even today such painting of the body is customary among a number of peoples. Unlike tattooing, this is carried out with water-soluble pigments (lime and others) with which symbols of joy, mourning, or ornamental decorations are painted on the body. Thus, for example, the painting of Indian warriors showed whether the tribe was on the warpath or not.

The Egyptians

The earliest Egyptian paintings were also carried out directly on rock. All reliefs were painted in several colors. Other Egyptian paintings were done on a ground of clay and mud from the Nile.

Numerous paintings on pottery show geometrical shapes, while others represent people, animals, and plants. The hieroglyphics with their many figure drawings were transformed into hieratic script in cursive form. Paper used for writing and painting was obtained from the papyrus shrub. It is assumed that plant juices were also used for the pigments. For mural paintings animal glue, resins, and wax acted as binding media, but vase paintings already show the use of rubber, honey, casein, and egg binders.

The Chinese and Japanese

Wood occupies a favored place in China and Japan. The architecture of these countries, in spite of many stone buildings, gave preference to wood, and this particularly furthered the style of wood construction. It also explains why, side

232

by side with frescoes, the wooden parts of buildings have been painted and lacquered in bright colors. In spite of the huge Wall of China, the Chinese have always been receptive to influences from western races; yet everything they observed was transformed into an original art. Apart from painting in pure India ink, their most important contribution was the technique of the colored woodcut, which in turn had a great influence on European painting.

To the Chinese and Japanese, whose art bears the same relationship as Greek art does to Roman in Europe, painting became a matter for the whole race. Favored by the technique of writing with a brush, the paintings of the Chinese and Japanese show a very sure mastery of the brush. People, animals, and landscapes are often transcribed with dreamlike certainty onto light paper and material (silk) grounds. Delicate yet decorative in effect, without emphasizing the cast shadow, these paintings are supported by complete mastery of bodily movement. The long, easily transportable scrolls of pictures take the place of wall paintings.

As pigments, thousands of years ago they used slightly soluble watercolors that contained protein, glue, and alum.

A speciality is Chinese lacquer painting, which has never been surpassed by any other race. Excavations have revealed lacquer paintings on wood whose origin dates back to the fourteenth century B. C.

India

Trade and traffic among peoples existed even in earliest times. Thus, important drugs and pigments came from the Orient to Europe in ancient times. Monumental cave paintings are known to us in India, dating from the first century B. C. The paintings were not made directly on the stone; it was first given a ground consisting of stone dust and rice chaff, and then smoothed with a thin layer of stucco. Painting took place on the still moist wall with opaque pigments which sometimes manifest a watercolorlike fluidity and transparency. As in all Oriental painting of this period. the lovingly worked-out motifs do not show any real light and shadow sections. As with the Chinese and Japanese, it appears as if space, the third dimension, had no influence on these paintings.

The main field of Indian art covers India and the island of Ceylon, and also includes Indochina and Indonesia, Tibet and Eastern Turkistan. The cave

temples are provided with extensive and extraordinarily rich mural paintings. Relief sculpture which is ornamental and rich in figures also supplements these paintings. In the sixteenth century the important miniature painting of the Indians makes its appearance, at the same time as definite industrial art (beaten work in metal and ivory carvings), this having extended down to our own day.

The paintings of Central and South America

Here we find mainly the various utensils of the Aztecs and Incas, whose paintings tell us about the use of pigments in these regions that once were so highly developed. A potter's wheel was not employed in making these utensils. Shaping was done by hand and bears witness to extraordinary skill and a fine artistic sense. Painting itself was restricted to a relatively narrow color scale. Red, black, and white are found chiefly, since they were clay pigments. Not only ornamentation was produced by the original inhabitants of the high plateaus in Central and South America, but figure representations occur as well, as with the races of the Old World.

The Mayas in particular have left excellent examples of handicrafts, dating from the first century B. C. to about 600 A. D. It is noteworthy that this ancient race had at its disposal a decided color scale. Paintings in orange, white, yellow, blue, grey, red, and brown were carried out with opaque colors coated with thick protective varnishes. Corresponding to the high place that textile art occupied in these areas thousands of years ago, we find here, as in their painting, a rich world of geometrical shapes as well as representations of animals and people.

234

The Greeks

The influence of Egyptian painting as well as the use of pigments and binding media is unmistakable in Greek painting. Coupled with these, they used geometrical figures in decorations of many types which, in the course of time, led to an independent Greek art of ornamentation. The painting of bright earthenware vessels was done with the help of tempera binding media in dark grey or black pigment. Other pigments used by the Greeks consisted mainly of white, ocher, red, and sometimes blue. While pigments ground with wax were used for external paintings to give improved durability, indoor paintings contain for the most part tempera binding media, namely, egg and rubber, as well as milk and glue.

The Etruscans

In Etruscan painting the compositional rhythms of Egyptian mural paintings can be recognized clearly. Greek influences are also unmistakable on the development of Etruscan style. The pigments for fresco technique were obtained from the local soil, and painting was carried out on white stucco. Most of these mural paintings have been found in the graves of Toscana, thousands of which have been laid open. Unfortunately, the effect of moisture has caused many of the findings to decay. All these paintings were carried out with the greatest care. The mural paintings in Corneto show very realistic scenes in fresh, almost impressionistic colors. The paintings of the Etruscans often reveal a thickly applied outline in black pigment. Black was likewise preferred in pottery, applied as a surface to jugs and vases which were then polished.

235

Pompeian Painting

The paintings preserved in the hot ashes of Vesuvius and the decorative works in palaces unearthed by excavation give us full information today about the techniques of this period, which also include the whole of Roman painting. Thus, the walls were covered by a plaster made from lime mixed with marble sand. This was followed by several layers of fine lime mortar, which were each applied over the still fresh lower layer. The pigments were then painted into the still moist uppermost layer of plaster. As a binding medium, Pompeian paintings used protein or glue, or a combination of egg white and pumice. Seven pigments were found in a "color shop" in this excavated city. Analysis showed them to be yellow ocher, brown-red ocher, a pink pigment that was no doubt a type of lake, Veronese green earth, a dough consisting of a blue pigment, and finally, as a white, a powder made from finely ground pumice stone. The use of all these pigments was confirmed by microscopic and micro-chemical tests of Pompeian plaster walls and their paintings. There were also red and yellow pigments which belong partly to the red ocher types of iron oxide and which must be partly of organic nature because they burn.

The Romans

The Pompeian technique of mural painting and also the decorative style of this center of art were of great influence on all the Roman provinces. Magnificent paintings of walls and no less richly decorated utensils on the Pompeian pattern were found everywhere. The painting of this period became ever more liberal and loose, the application of the brush ever thicker, and the total effect of these works on a white ground is in some cases absolutely impressionistic (catacombs in Rome). These bold color symphonies were carried out in tempera technique and have not been preserved as well as the panel paintings of the time, which already show the use of linseed oil besides beeswax and resins.

236

Byzantine Painting (300–1200 A. D.)

Centering in ancient Byzantium (Constantinople), the present-day Istanbul, this stylistic epoch shows, apart from numerous monumental buildings, a great many paintings and mosaics. As in the painting of the ancient Egyptians, the representation of figures lacks a shadow effect and a three-dimensional emphasis of space. In contrast, there was now a movement away from the pure profile view of figures to a frontal view. One feature of Byzantine art is the marked stylization which follows architectural requirements. In cases where preference was not, as in Ravenna, given to mosaic pictures, painting was carried out al fresco, that is, on still moist plaster. Plant fibres were mixed with the plaster, as in ancient Egypt, in order to keep the sometimes huge areas fresh while painting, this mixture inducing a slow drying process. Investigations have shown that the masters of Byzantine painting carried out their preliminary drawings without transfers. This was done directly with the brush by means of outlining with red pigment. Ornamental details and decorations were often applied with tempera pigments (egg and rubber) after completing the al fresco painting.

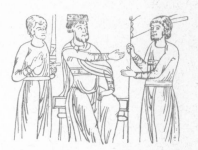

The Middle Ages

Oil grounding has generally been used for industrial work in painting since the twelfth century. Oil pigment technique occupied a large place when wood was used for buildings, a method favored in the Middle Ages. Panelwork façades and timber ceilings were painted, with the addition of linseed oil, and the wooden panels used as supports for paintings were grounded, using linseed oil, care being taken that the layers of grounding had a slightly increasing oil

237

content from the lowest to the uppermost layer. Later, when building in stone supplanted the use of wood more and more, the stone reliefe also were painted with oil pigment. The permanence of these paintings was, however, very limited.

When the panel picture became more and more popular, because of the relatively small wall areas in Gothic buildings, it was principally the brothers Hubert and Jan van Eyck who, by the addition of oil (egg-oil tempera), created a combination in tempera and oil, so that the invention of oil pigment technique is largely ascribed to them. This new technique was used for the first time by the van Eyck brothers when painting the altar in Ghent. The technique is characterized down to the present day by great permanence and freshness of the colors, which found suitable support in the fine, superimposed, thin layers of glaze.

Renaissance Painting

The greatest masters of occidental painting belong to this period, which saw the rise of the sciences, of new discoveries and inventions. The artist became equal to the greatmen of the world, and himself strove towards new goals and knowledge. This period, nevertheless, has no real importance as regards the technical improvement of contemporary painting. Occupied with the brilliance of his performance, the genius found no time to study his materials thoroughly. Thus, for example, **The Last Supper,** which Leonardo da Vinci painted in oil pigments on a wall, very soon began to show signs of decay. The advantages of fresco technique, with which Giotto almost two hundred years earlier had acquired a foremost place in painting, were more and more lost to the Renaissance painters, and gradually disappeared at the beginning of the seventeenth century.

On the other hand, canvas replaced the wooden ground for painting at the beginning of the fifteenth century. The picture could thus be transported more

238

easily and became, in the course of time, less dependent on a wall that was fixed to one spot. Paintings on canvas are, however, more prone to destruction, since the thin support of the picture is also subject to attack by moisture on its reverse side. Paintings on canvas were often destroyed, there being no heating and drying facilities in the modern sense at that time.

Baroque Painting

Apart from religious paintings, in which oil color dominated as the material, we find casein lime painting, which had already been known to the Greeks. This technique was used for many wall and ceiling paintings of this period.

In addition, history and genre paintings, landscapes, as well as paintings of animals and still life were raised to independent categories of art.

Independent schools of painting evolved in the Netherlands, Italy, France, and Spain. Even more than during the Renaissance, the panel painting found its way into the homes of ordinary citizens and into places of business. It adorned the walls of collectors, and the concept of the picture- or art-dealer was created. A colored ground was often used in Baroque paintings, in gray-red, brown-gray, and the like.

Painting in recent times

Very little has changed in principle as regards color, that is, its material nature, origin, and the necessary binding media. Essentially, people today work with the same materials, and even the methods of painting have not changed to any great extent. If we disregard developments and advances in the chemical industry whose greatest and, in fact, revolutionary innovations lie in the manufacture of varnish, it is man himself who has changed since the beginning of all cultural creation. It is more the method of expression that has altered; it is more the views on art that have changed and less its materials, which have preserved their validity in principle throughout all periods.

Decorative sketch in two colors

Twentieth century art, in contrast to that of earlier centuries, shows a decided antinaturalistic tendency. The turning away from nature is common to all modern trends. They all, nevertheless, require color, which is the basic element of their creation. One may agree with the contemporary view of art, which cannot be called new in all its forms, or one can devote oneself to nature, which has not by any means been fully explored in all its variety and secrets. Artistic creation, however, must always conform with the laws of harmony, which are, in the final analysis, a part of vast nature, as is man himself.